David Hare

Twayne's English Authors Series

Kinley E. Roby, Editor

Northeastern University

TEAS 480

DAVID HARE
Photography by John Haynes
Courtesy of the Royal National Theatre

David Hare

By Joan FitzPatrick Dean

University of Missouri–Kansas City

Twayne Publishers • Boston
A Division of G. K. Hall & Co.

David Hare
Joan FitzPatrick Dean

Copyright 1990 by G. K. Hall & Co.
All rights reserved.
Published by Twayne Publishers
A division of G. K. Hall & Co.
70 Lincoln Street
Boston, Massachusetts 02111

Copyediting supervised by Barbara Sutton.
Book production by Gabrielle B. McDonald.
Book design by Barbara Anderson.
Typeset in 11 pt. Garamond
by Huron Valley Graphics of Ann Arbor, Michigan.

First published 1990.
10 9 8 7 6 5 4 3 2 1

Library of Congress Cataloging-in-Publication Data

Dean, Joan FitzPatrick
    David Hare / by Joan FitzPatrick Dean.
        p.   cm. — (Twayne's English authors series ; TEAS 480)
    Includes bibliographical references.
    ISBN 0-8057-6997-8 (alk. paper)
    1. Hare, David, 1947– —Criticism and interpretation.
I. Title.   II. Series.
PR6058.A678Z65   1990
822'.914—dc20   90-33018
                                                                              CIP

To my daughters, Margaret and Flannery Cashill

Contents

About the Author

Professor of English and director of honors, Joan FitzPatrick Dean teaches modern and Renaissance literature at the University of Missouri— Kansas City. She received her Ph.D. from Purdue University in 1975. Her publications on such contemporary British dramatists as Peter Shaffer, Tom Stoppard, and Joe Orton have appeared in *Modern Drama, Theatre Journal,* and other journals. The author of *Tom Stoppard: Comedy as a Moral Matrix* (1981), she was a Fulbright lecturer at the Université de Nancy (France) in 1982—83. She has studied or taught in Dublin, London, and Lima, Peru.

Preface

David Hare is a writer who resists categorization. His plays are satirical, but he is not primarily a satirist. He has been identified as a political playwright from the beginning of his career, yet his characters are rarely doctrinaire, always complex.

Offering a potent if unflattering view of Britain over the past forty-five years, Hare draws a composite portrait of the British that focuses on repression, disillusionment, and despair. His plays sometimes exasperate reviewers and critics because they depict specifically British or American characters as if an individual can sum up an entity as complex as Britain or America. Oddly, foreign reviewers often respond more favorably to his works than British critics do. And despite the fact that Hare's primary subject is the British, his works travel surprisingly well, certainly in the English-speaking world. His plays have been performed in the United States for nearly as long as he has been writing them. *A Map of the World* was first performed in Australia at the Adelaide Festival. And probably his most impressive award, the Golden Bear, came from the Berlin Film Festival.

Critics sometimes attack Hare either for submerging his political and social commentary within all too familiar dramatic forms or for creating characters that speak only as ideological mouthpieces. Criticized as both pedantic and puzzling, both too oblique and too obvious, Hare's works frustrate many critics. The coexistence of the comic and the calamitous is clearly one source of uneasiness for Hare's audience. His humor is invariably barbed, Brechtian in the best sense of the term, because the audience cannot laugh until it has learned. There is, too, a temptation to interpret the plays as exercises in camp—to overstress their satirical dimension and to overplay their often caustic wit. But to yield to that temptation is to miss the fundamental humanity of Hare's characters.

Unquestionably, Hare disconcerts his audience and does so deliberately. The ambivalence of his protagonists makes it difficult to draw unequivocal conclusions about his works. In *Plenty*, the protagonist, Susan Traherne, elicits contempt as well as compassion, repulsion as well as respect. Characters in *Teeth 'n' Smiles, Licking Hitler, Dreams of*

Leaving, and other works seem to squander their not inconsiderable talents. Especially troublesome are the many characters, most often villains, who successfully manage to delude themselves as well as their victims. Often Hare evokes a particular style or genre only to deny the audience the predictable conclusions it anticipates. In *Knuckle,* a work inspired by Ross Macdonald's novels, everything points to its protagonist as a hero; yet the would-be hero eventually capitulates with no sense of loss or regret. And, in the words of one reviewer, the film version of *Plenty* "denies us some of the melodramatic payoffs we're conditioned to expect in movies with troubled heroines." Similarly, *A Map of the World* creates suspense about a debate between two characters that never takes place. As soon as Hare's audience expects the predictable, it takes too much for granted.

In some ways Hare's career epitomizes the movement of the arts in Britain since the tumultuous 1960s. Perhaps this is most evident in the changes in the audience Hare attracts. Beginning on the Fringe in the late 1960s, Hare wrote for a small company that often performed for small audiences in remote places. In at least one instance in the 1960s, only one person showed up for a performance by Hare's Portable Theatre Company. But by the late 1980s Hare had moved from the Fringe to the very heart of British theater. Not only are his stage plays and films now seen by an international audience, and not only is Hare one of the seven company directors at Britain's National Theatre, but Hare and that lone spectator, Howard Brenton, have written the second longest-running production mounted by the National Theatre, *Pravda.*

Like many British playwrights born in the 1940s, Hare has always been interested in drama as a vehicle for political commentary. Hare has helped to redefine the mainstream of British theater by examining political and social concerns in works more popular than polemic. His audience has changed perhaps more than his plays have. Because of the impact of companies like the Portable Theatre Company and the Joint Stock Company, British audiences in particular have come to expect that political issues are as integral to drama as they are to life. Presuming many Americans are largely unfamiliar with recent British history, I present some background material in this study that may strike British readers as obvious or simplistic. In most cases, however, understanding the context of Hare's works is essential to understanding the works themselves.

Perhaps the single feature of Hare's works that most clearly distinguishes him from his contemporaries is the notion that idealism remains a possibility. Despite the cynicism, despite the madness, David Hare always pursues the ideals that elude us all.

Joan FitzPatrick Dean

University of Missouri–Kansas City

Acknowledgments

Excerpts from *The Great Exhibition, Slag, Knuckle, Fanshen, Teeth 'n' Smiles, Plenty, Dreams of Leaving, Wetherby, Saigon: Year of the Cat,* and *A Map of the World* by David Hare are reprinted by permission of Faber & Faber Ltd.

Excerpts from *Brassneck* and *Pravda: A Fleet Street Comedy* by David Hare and Howard Brenton are reprinted by permission of Methuen London Ltd.

Excerpts from *The Bay Nice and Wrecked Eggs* and *The Secret Rapture* by David Hare are reprinted by permission of Margaret Ramsey Ltd. All rights whatsoever in these plays are strictly reserved and application for performance, etc., should be made before rehearsal to Margaret Ramsey Ltd., 14a Goodwin's Court, St. Martin's Lane, London, WC2. No performance may be given unless a license has been obtained.

The Missouri London Program facilitated this work by providing the opportunity for me to spend a semester in London in 1986 and another two weeks in 1989. I enjoyed the support of the University of Missouri–Kansas City through funds from the Dean of Arts and Sciences, the Office of Research Administration, Research Incentive Funds, the University Associates, and the Weldon Spring Humanities Seminar Endowment.

I am grateful to Vicki Rawdon, Fe Gatapia, and the staff of the Belmont School.

I wish to thank Professors Linda E. Voigts and W. Clark Hendley, Jr. for locating and forwarding articles about Hare from the British press. Unlike any clipping service, they never failed to provide adequate citations. To them and several other colleagues at the University of Missouri–Kansas City I am grateful for their encouragement.

I owe a special debt to my mentor, Professor Albert E. Kalson of Purdue University, who read an early draft and made many valuable suggestions.

Finally, I want to thank Jack who, among other things, always encourages me to choose the active over the passive.

Chronology

1947   David Hare born 5 June in St. Leonards, Sussex, England.

1968   Receives master's degree in English from Jesus College, Cambridge. Cofounds and is director of the Portable Theatre Company.

1969   Serves as literary manager at the Royal Court Theatre, London. *How Brophy Made Good,* directed by Hare and Tony Bicât, produced at Oval House, London; published in *Gambit.*

1970   *Slag,* produced at the Hampstead Theatre Club. *What Happened to Blake?* produced by the Portable Theatre. Becomes resident dramatist at the Royal Court Theatre. Wins *Evening Standard Award* for most promising playwright for *Slag.* Hare marries theatrical agent Margaret Mathieson with whom he has three children.

1971   Collaborates with six other playwrights to write *Lay By.* Two-minute play "Deathshead" performed at the Edinburgh Festival.

1972   *England's Ireland* first produced in Amsterdam and later at the Round House, directed by Hare, in London. Portable Theatre files for bankruptcy. *The Great Exhibition* produced at the Hampstead Theatre Club.

1973   *Brassneck,* a collaboration with Howard Brenton, opens 19 September at Nottingham Playhouse, directed by Hare. Becomes resident dramatist at Nottingham Playhouse. Cofounds the Joint Stock Theatre Group. *Man above Men* aired on BBC-1. Visits Saigon.

1974   *Knuckle* produced 29 January at the Oxford Playhouse; opens 4 March in West End at the Comedy Theatre; published by Faber & Faber.

1975   Is first dramatist to win the John Llewellyn Rhys Prize. Television version of *Knuckle* airs in America. *Teeth 'n' Smiles,* directed by the author, opens at Royal Court Theatre. Television version of *Brassneck* airs in Britain. *Fanshen,* produced by Joint Stock Theatre Group and directed by Hare, opens at ICA on 21 April, and at the Hampstead Theatre Club on 12 August.

1978   *Plenty,* directed by Hare, produced at the Lyttelton Theatre on 7
       April. *Licking Hitler,* directed by Hare, televised and published;
       wins BAFTA Best Play of the Year Award. Visits California on
       U.S./U.K. Bicentennial Fellowship.

1980   *Dreams of Leaving,* directed by Hare, airs in Britain. Hare and
       Margaret Mathieson divorce.

1981   *Saigon: Year of the Cat,* directed by Stephen Frears, televised and
       published.

1983   *A Map of the World,* directed by Hare, produced at the Adelaide
       Festival and the National Theatre. *Plenty* receives New York
       Critics Circle Award for best foreign play.

1985   *Wetherby,* film directed by Hare, wins Golden Bear Award at the
       Berlin Film Festival. *London Standard, City Limits,* and *Plays
       and Players* all name *Pravda,* written in collaboration with Bren-
       ton and directed by Hare at the National Theatre, as best play
       for the year.

1986   *The Bay at Nice* and *Wrecked Eggs* performed on a double bill
       directed by Hare at the National Theatre 9 September. Hare
       directs Anthony Hopkins in the title role of *King Lear* at the
       National Theatre on 10 December.

1987   The unpublished opera *The Knife* (music by Nick Bicât, book by
       Hare, lyrics by Tim Rose Price, directed by Hare) produced at
       the Public/Newman Theater by the New York Shakespeare Festi-
       val in February.

1988   *The Secret Rapture,* directed by Howard Davies, opens at the
       National Theatre.

1989   The film *Paris by Night* released commercially in England. The
       film *Strapless* appears in the New York Film Festival and the
       Telluride (Colorado) Film Festival. Hare's direction of *The Secret
       Rapture* on Broadway.

Chapter One
A Life in the Theater

David Hare was born on 5 June 1947 in St. Leonards, near Hastings, Sussex, the only son of Clifford and Agnes Hare. His family moved some ten miles to Bexhill-on-Sea, a small seaside town, "an extremely geriatric sort of place,"[1] as Hare describes it, when he was five years old. Hare's father, a sailor and purser, was often away from his family for long periods.

On scholarship, Hare attended Lancing College, a public school in West Sussex, whose most famous alumnus, Evelyn Waugh, describes the school in *A Little Learning* and fictionalizes it in "Charles Ryder's School Days." At Lancing, a "very decadent and art-oriented" place that he "enjoyed . . . a great deal,"[2] Hare first met Christopher Hampton, whose play *Total Eclipse* Hare would direct in London in 1981. Hare went on to Jesus College, Cambridge, to study under Raymond Williams.[3] At Cambridge, reportedly enduring "the unhappiest years of his life,"[4] Hare read English and received an M.A. in 1968, a watershed year for student political activism. In France, the United States, and, to a far lesser extent, Britain often violent demonstrations capped an unprecedented wave of student protest. Hare's political and social consciousness, evident even in his teens, was shaped by these now celebrated years of social turmoil.

During the first twenty-one years of Hare's life, Britain underwent far-reaching changes in almost every aspect of life. Emerging victorious from World War II, Britain had good reason to hope in the future. But if the postcolonial Britain of Hare's youth promised peace, prosperity, and a classless society that would provide for the common welfare, what it produced was economic crisis, inept diplomacy, and a still rigidly stratified society. At the time of Hare's birth, unlike any time during World War II, even bread was rationed in England.[5] That sustained austerity becomes the correlative of an emotional and spiritual privation, especially in works like *Plenty* and *Licking Hitler* that are set in the 1940s and 1950s. Hare's plays chronicle the postwar decades with reference not only to the postcolonial decline of Britain but also to what the economist Peter Calvocoressi identifies as the most dangerous weaknesses of Britain: inequality and secretiveness.[6] Hare describes himself as "forced up through the class system."[7] His consciousness of the British class system which figures in all of his works that deal with the British, was doubtless heightened by his own background. No less important than his modest origins and his privileged educational background is Hare's class consciousness and leftist political orientation.

After graduating from Cambridge, Hare first worked for A. B. Pathé, the film company, where in only a few months he saw the entire stock of Pathé Pictorials. Decades later Hare admitted: "I've always wanted to work in feature films since I was a boy."[8] His career as a playwright, however, began inadvertently. Hare recalls writing very little while at Cambridge and in 1978 acknowledged that he "became a writer by default, to fill in the gaps, to work on areas of the fresco which were simply ignored."[9] Since 1968 Hare has earned an impressive reputation not only as a prolific writer but also as a theater and film director, theater founder, and literary manager.

Dramatic Background

In 1954 Kenneth Tynan decried the British drama's prevalent genre, the Loamshire play, as invalid:

Its setting is a country house in what used to be called Loamshire but is now, as a heroic tribute to realism, sometimes called Berkshire. Except when someone must sneeze, or be murdered, the sun invariably shines. The inhabitants belong to a social class derived partly from romantic novels and partly from the playwright's vision of the leisured life he will lead after the play is a success— this being the only effort of imagination he is called on to make. Joys and sorrows are giggles and whimpers: the crash of denunciation dwindles into "Oh, stuff, Mummy!" and "Oh, really Daddy!" And so grim is the continuity of these things that the foregoing paragraph might have been written at any time during the last thirty years.[10]

But within months of Tynan's lament, British drama was galvanized from without and within by the arrival of startling foreign imports and the emergence not only of Britain's Angry Young Men but of the production operations that would sustain and encourage generations of British playwrights.

Beginning with the watershed events of 1955 and 1956—John Osborne's *Look Back in Anger,* the visit of Bertolt Brecht's Berliner Ensemble, the first English production of Samuel Beckett's *Waiting for Godot*—British theater experienced a revival that it continues to enjoy. In 1955, when "there were no major theatre companies willing to take on experimental work,"[11] George Devine founded the English Stage Company, a company devoted to "creating a new body of English writing for the theatre and creating an audience for the writing."[12] The playwrights Devine produced—John Osborne (b. 1929), John Arden (b. 1930), and Arnold Wesker (b. 1932), identified as the Angry Young Men (Ann Jellicoe [b. 1927], Shelagh Delaney [b. 1939], and Joan Littlewood [b. 1914] should be mentioned as Angry Young Women)—were the so-called first wave of innovative postwar British playwrights. By the end of the decade Harold Pinter (b. 1930) enlarged the range of contemporary British drama in apolitical directions in plays that although owing much to continental influences like the theater of the absurd, were distinctly British in setting and ambience. There followed what John Russell Taylor calls the second wave[13]—including Peter Nichols (b. 1927), Tom Stoppard (b. 1937), Joe Orton (b. 1933), and Peter Shaffer (b. 1926)—dramatists born before World War II who were less angry and less politically motivated but no less talented. The renewal begun in 1955–56 had made the theater attractive to political as well as apolitical writers. As Stoppard says, "after 1956 everybody of my age who wanted to write, wanted to write plays."[14]

Britain's preeminence in drama solidified in the 1960s and 1970s: the Royal Shakespeare Company established a London base at the Aldwych Theatre; Arts Council funding, which stood at £675,000 in 1952, rose to £37 million in 1976; the number of regional repertory companies more than doubled between 1956 and 1976; in the 1970s both the National Theatre and the Royal Shakespeare Company found permanent multitheater homes in London.[15] By 1973 more than half of the tourists visiting London would identify the theater as one of the city's greatest attractions.[16]

Playwrights of Hare's generation, many of whom were born during or shortly after the war and began writing plays in the late 1960s, constitute a third wave of dramatists who have reshaped the British stage. Once dubbed "the wild bunch" by John Peter,[17] this third wave includes Christopher Hampton (b. 1948), Snoo Wilson (b. 1948), Stephen Poliakoff (b. 1952), Caryl Churchill (b. 1938), Trevor Griffiths (b. 1935), and Howard Brenton (b. 1942). They are a well-educated, university-trained generation of playwrights committed to

socialist politics and to a theater that accommodates their political
consciousness.

The Portable Theatre Company

In 1968 Hare and Tony Bicât, who also studied English literature at
Cambridge in the late 1960s, founded the touring company Portable
Theatre, to move theater out of the West End "to places where it normally didn't go."[18] Untainted by the commercialism of the theatrical
world, Bicât and Hare envisioned a more powerful, "one-to-one relationship between an actor and an audience."[19] The Portable Theatre was
committed not only to the liberal cause and a populist ideal for drama but
also to the production of new plays by unknown playwrights.

In retrospect, the Portable can now be seen as part of the larger
movement of British Fringe theater that sought alternatives to commercial theater in the late 1960s. That same year the Arts Lab opened in
Drury Lane; other mobile companies like the Freehold and the People
Show took to the road; Charles Marowitz's Open Space Theatre, Inter-
Action, and others also emerged. At the time, however, Hare did not
even know of the existence of groups like La Mama. The passage of time
has not diminished the importance of such Fringe experiments. Peter
Ansorge, for instance, writes that "between 1968 and 1973 [the new
migrant troupes] played as vital a part in the life of our subsidized
theatre as the Royal Court, National or Royal Shakespeare Company."[20]
As the playwrights whose earliest works were performed by companies
like the Portable—Howard Brenton, Trevor Griffiths, Brian Clark,
Snoo Wilson, Stephen Poliakoff, and Hare himself—continue to produce plays, the reputation of those companies continues to grow. The
Portable and groups like it were instrumental not only in bringing
theater to previously isolated communities, but also in presenting the
works of a new generation of playwrights who were at the time noncom-
mercial and often overtly political. But the Fringe groups in the late
1960s were most important for their irreverence toward the establishment and for their demolition of the notion that the theater was inherently limited to certain subjects and styles.

Given Hare's academic and literary background, his adaptations of
biographies in his earliest plays are hardly surprising. Hare and Bicât
based one of the Portable's first projects, *Inside Out* (1968), on Franz
Kafka's diaries. Later, the lives of Strindberg and Blake were sources for
the Portable's works. In contrast to other theater companies, the Porta-

ble soon established a reputation as the "nearest group to a 'writers' theatre' on the fringe."[21]

Two events from those days with the Portable Theatre have proved especially serendipitous to Hare's theatrical career. The first was the evening that the sole member of the audience for a Portable production was Howard Brenton. Brenton steered the Portable Theatre away from its literary preoccupations and toward contemporary subjects. He and Hare would eventually collaborate on four plays. More immediately, Brenton offered *Christie in Love*, a play based on the life of a notorious British criminal, that Hare directed first for the Portable and then in 1970 for the Royal Court. The second event was Snoo Wilson's failure to deliver a play commissioned by the Portable. Forced to come up with a play in short order, Hare wrote *How Brophy Made Good*, a slapdash effort that nonetheless gave Hare sufficient recognition as a playwright to gain access to the Royal Court Theatre and to come to the attention of the producer Michael Codron.[22]

That same year, 1969, Christopher Hampton—then resident dramatist at the Royal Court—was instrumental in effecting Hare's appointment as literary manager. Over the next three years Hare remedied any deficiencies in his theatrical background by reading some nine hundred plays submitted to the Royal Court and seeing another two to three hundred plays produced. That immersion in theater resulted in a command of dramatic techniques, and perhaps subdued the inclination toward self-conscious technical experiments that characterized much of the Fringe.

Hare as Director

Like Harold Pinter, Hare is important in the English-speaking world not only because he writes theatrical works and screenplays, but also because he directs plays and films. As a director, Hare has worked primarily for the theater, but he has also directed several of his own works for television and the works that he has written exclusively for film: *Wetherby, Paris by Night* (1989), and *Strapless* (1989).

Hare's career as a stage director indicates his close association with playwrights of his own generation. Peter Hall records in his diaries that Hare indicated to him little desire to direct the classics.[23] In addition to directing his own works, he has directed plays by Howard Brenton (*Christie in Love* [1969], *Fruit* [1970], *Weapons of Happiness* [1976]) and Snoo Wilson (*Blow Job* [1971] and *The Pleasure Principle* [1973]), both of whom he has also collaborated with. Although most attracted to the works of playwrights of his own generation, including Christopher Hampton, in 1986 Hare directed Shakespeare's *King Lear* at the National Theatre, where since the mid-1980s he has directed one of the ensemble teams.

Critical Reputation

In more than twenty years of involvement in the theater, Hare's remarkable talents have garnered a variety of awards and recognitions. The London *Evening Standard* honored Hare as the most promising new playwright of 1970 for *Slag*. Four years later, as the author of *Knuckle,* Hare was the first dramatist to win the John Llewellyn Rhys Memorial Prize, presented to the most promising literary work written by a Briton under the age of thirty. *Licking Hitler,* the 1978 television play written and directed by Hare, won the British Academy of Film and Television Award for the best play of the year. In 1978 the *Sunday Times* (London) elevated Hare from "the wild bunch" (Griffiths, Poliakoff, Brenton, David Edgar, Heathcote Williams, Howard Barker, and Barrie Keeffe) to the company of Osborne, Stoppard, Pinter, David Storey, Arden, Peter Barnes, and Alan Bennett.[24] *Plenty* received the 1983 New York Critics Circle Award for best foreign play. In 1985 *Wetherby,* written and directed by Hare, won the Golden Bear Award at the Berlin Film Festival. That same year the London *Evening Standard, City Limits,* and *Plays and Players* all named *Pravda,* Hare's collaboration with Howard Brenton, the best play of the year.

Despite Hare's acclaim as a director and a writer for film, television, and the stage, serious critical assessment of his work remains slight. By the mid-1970s critics found it convenient to group Hare with aggressively, overtly political playwrights like Edward Bond, John Arden, and Howard Brenton. In 1975 Peter Ansorge stressed the satirical and parodic nature of Hare's works, calling him "certainly the brightest literary satirist in the underground."[25] The next year John Peter described Hare and his collaborators as "marauding moralists."[26] In 1980 Catherine Itzin described Hare as "one of the more radical figures in the British theatre of the seventies."[27] But to speak of Hare today primarily as a satirist or as a politically radical dramatist is clearly misleading.

Some of the critical assessments of Hare are tinged by the implication that he has compromised himself by becoming part of the mainstream or establishment. In damning the original London production of

Plenty with the faintest praise, W. Stephen Gilbert incorrectly predicted Hare's sellout: "I have this notion that we'll next hear of him as the author (and perhaps the director) of a Hollywood movie for Faye Dunaway."[28] In the early 1980s Simon Trussler wrote that Hare "has continued somewhat disarmingly to straddle the fence which conventionally divides 'alternative' theatre from the institutional variety."[29] Hare's own view is that once a playwright can make his own way in commercial theater, he has an obligation to free up the subsidized theaters for the works of new, unestablished playwrights.[30]

In 1984 John Bull offered a solid reading that stressed the political dimension of Hare's work by identifying his focus on "central characters [who] are misfits, living out their disillusionment through the dismal unrolling of post-1939 British history."[31] Despite Bull's analysis, three years later Colin Chambers and Mike Prior in *Playwrights' Progress* pigeonholed Hare as a dramatist of the 1970s who could not make the transition to the 1980s.[32]

Feminist readings of Hare's work are oddly disappointing. In reviews feminists sometimes fault Hare because his female protagonists end unhappily. In reviewing the film version of *Plenty,* for instance, Pam Cook criticized Hare not only for "obsessively repeating" a simplistic version of Britain but also "a retrograde use of female characters as vehicles for [his] own hang-ups."[33] Michelene Wandor offered this unlikely reading of *Teeth 'n' Smiles:* "The man as artist is vindicated and he will have to find another woman to interpret his art."[34] Not only does the man in question care more for this woman than for his art, but he is in no way vindicated. Wandor's 1987 study, *Look Back in Gender,* entirely ignored Susan Traherne in *Plenty*—arguably "one of the best roles written for an actress since Brecht's *Mutter Courage.*"[35] Critical estimation of Hare's work remains decidedly mixed. Indeed, he is an author who resists labels and whose works are as diverse in style as in substance.

Kenneth Tynan broadly but insightfully divides contemporary British playwrights into two camps: the "hairy men" and the "smooth men."[36] The smooth men, like Tom Stoppard and Harold Pinter, are stylists, elegant wordsmiths, who manipulate the relationship between theater and reality. Hairy men, on the other hand, are socially committed dramatists whose plays relentlessly insist upon the primacy of social and political causes. Ronald Hayman groups Hare among those playwrights professing "the politics of hatred." In 1979 Hayman argued that "by the middle Seventies socialist realism had become the

norm . . . our socialist realist playwrights are on the whole less interested in being artists than in precipitating social change."[37] Although
there is some truth in Hayman's generalization, it is especially inappro-
priate in Hare's case. Because of Hare's involvement with the Portable
Theatre and later with the Joint Stock Theatre Group, his collaborative
associations with playwrights such as Brenton, Wilson, and Griffiths,
and the social and political dimensions of his work, Hare was initially
perceived as a very hairy playwright. Yet Hare's plays are not primarily
didactic vehicles that assault the audience's sensibilities with dramatiza-
tions of social injustices. In the past twenty years Hare has mastered
effective techniques of dramatizing the relationship between individuals and historical events that is today his hallmark. In contrast with the
truly hairy men of British theater, such as his collaborators, Hare
portrays psychologically complex characters often in intensely romantic
relationships set against social and political backgrounds in dramatically compelling ways.

In interviews Hare reveals himself as a playwright much aware of the
possibilities of theatrical forms. Many of his plays are comparatively
straightforward and conventional in their dramaturgy. They are not
self-reflexive, nor primarily concerned with the stage as a metaphor for
life; instead they embody Hare's belief in the primacy of content: "It's
always the content of the work that determines everything"[38]—a restate-
ment of the notion that form follows function. Although many of his
works are stylish, dramatic form in itself is vastly less important to
Hare than themes and characterization.

Recurrent Themes and Characters

Infused with idealism and its attendant disillusionment, Hare's plays
reflect a profound sense of loss and disappointment. Like many of his
contemporaries, Hare responds to the status of Britain in its postcolonial contraction by seeking out new possibilities—often political
possibilities—for the theater. But unlike any of his contemporaries,
Hare portrays romance and idealism as convincingly as he depicts corruption and cynicism. He goes beyond the immediate political implications of being British in the late twentieth century to address the
personal dilemma of living with those political implications. Invariably
his plays chronicle the state of British society with an unremitting focus
on the bonds between the private and the public, the personal and the
political.

In 1978 Hare said of his work: "I try to show the English their history. I write tribal pieces, trying to show how people behaved on this island, off this continental shelf, in this century. How this Empire vanished, how these ideals died."[39] Hare's principal themes—the ubiquity of corruption and the death of ideals—are cast in what, until very recently, has been his primary subject: the exploration of the British character. Especially for the British women Hare creates, corruption and disillusionment offer only the choice between madness and complicity.

Recurrent themes and character types not only link his early plays, but also anticipate Hare's mature work. Unquestionably, Hare's social consciousness, especially in regard to Britain's postcolonial status and its class structure, appears in every play. To be sure, Hare sees capitalism as enslavement of the lower and middle classes, but what truly horrifies him is the ready acceptance of a reprehensible system: "Consciousness has been raised in this country for a good many years now and we seem further from radical political change than at anytime in my life. The traditional function of the radical artist—'Look at those Borgias; look at this bureaucracy,'—has been undermined. We have looked. We have seen. And we have not changed. A pervasive cynicism paralyses public life."[40] This paralysis in public life often manifests itself in the entropy of his characters. The intimate and often terrifying implications of political realities move many of his characters beyond entropy, to despair or madness.

Central to the early plays, especially in their relationship with his later works, is the role of Hare's idealists. *Slag, The Great Exhibition, Brassneck,* and, to a lesser extent, *Fanshen,* depict characters committed to social reform. Yet that very commitment virtually assures their eventual disillusionment. Idealists continue to populate his later plays, although their idealism is more rarely expressed in explicitly political terms.

Chapter Two

Early Works

How Brophy Made Good

> I was influenced by some of the French situationists (the situa-
> tionists were very important to the May 1968 students). The
> situationists describe our world as "the society of the spectacle."
> There is a screen called public life which is reported on the telly
> and in the newspapers. This version of public life is a spectacle, it
> operates within its own laws. It's a vast, intricate confidence
> game![1]

So said not David Hare but Howard Brenton in reference to his play
Fruit, which Hare directed in 1970. Yet what Brenton says about *Fruit*
is equally applicable to *How Brophy Made Good.*

With only a few days in which to write *How Brophy Made Good,* Hare
turned to a very topical source—newspaper and television coverage of a
tumultuous summer—for his subject. *Brophy* was written in 1969 at a
time of increasing social unrest in Britain. Deteriorating relationships
between Catholics and Protestants in Northern Ireland, Enoch Powell's
inflammatory statements about immigration policies, protests against
the Vietnam War, mounting inflation, and labor disputes—all brought
demonstrators into the streets to vie for media attention. But Hare's
first play deals more with the way in which events are reported than
with the events themselves.

Waxing rhetorical on the subject, Leonard Cook, a socialist leader in
How Brophy Made Good, says: "We have sweated through the hottest,
most dispiriting summer of a nation's life. The sweat has poured from
us like a burst dam."[2] Against a background of riots and death in
London's streets, the liberal leadership searches for a gimmick to capture media attention, while Brophy, a media commentator, makes good
for himself by making light of the liberal cause.

Brophy fulfills Andy Warhol's prophecy that in the future everyone
will be famous for fifteen minutes. Born to a Cockney working-class
family, Brophy "smile[s] up from the bottom of the capitalist shit-

heap" (87) and rises to national celebrity as a media personality. As a cynical commentator on contemporary life, he enjoys the pleasures of success, including an affair with Smiles, a BBC announcer. But after basking in his media celebrity, Brophy falls from public favor and simply disappears.

Hare is always vague about exactly *how* Brophy made good. Using the "mediaspeak" of the television commentator, Smiles says of him: "Distinctively of our times, labelled tough and dynamic Brophy forges upward. . . . He performs acts of an unspecific nature and of an undeniable brilliance. The critics applaud his daring. His bravado and exuberance stun imagination. He is a star" (88). As Marshall McLuhan wrote in his analysis of the media, the medium is the message, and Brophy is the perfect McLuhanesque "cool" personality. Ideally suited to television, Brophy does not burn with the ardor of a social reformer and mocks those who do.

Everyone in *Brophy* recognizes the importance of manipulating the media. Leonard, who is described as the direct descendant of Marx, Lenin, Trotsky, and Stalin, announces from his soapbox that "Media are the first target of the socialist revolution" (104). Leonard loves the spotlight at least as much as Brophy does, but his opinions are too dogmatic to inspire celebrity.

Brophy, first the media analyst, himself becomes the subject of media analysis. As the media interview, document, and glamorize him, Brophy becomes news. He carves a niche for himself as an entertainer, detached from the social causes on which he comments. Recognizing his talent to entertain as soon as he "stopped taking people seriously" (106), he accepts the public as "suckers" (98) and sees his job as "to make people happy" (97). Parodying the clichés of BBC reportage, he says: "In these times of moral decay I stand for something rather important. There's a gritty integrity about me" (99). In fact, his gritty integrity seems to lie in his candid solipsism. Interviewed by Smiles on television as to what he enjoys, Brophy unabashedly answers, "I like fucking you . . . food and thinking about myself" (107). In both scenes 2 and 8, Brophy makes obscene, threatening phone calls to complete strangers in order to malign Peter, his closest rival for the affection of Smiles. These phone calls stand as an emblem for Brophy's commentaries: detached, cynical, and manipulative.

Brophy's principal target is the cloying sincerity and verbosity of the liberal rhetoric epitomized by the posters Leonard and Peter design: "CAPITALISM IS REIFICATION" and "THE FORCES OF REVI-

SIONISM MUST NEVER, WHATEVER THE TEMPTATIONS, BE
ALLOWED TO HOLD BACK THE FORCES OF PROGRESS" (119–
20). Here, too, the medium is the message, and the liberal rhetoric is
easily ridiculed by Brophy.

Peter, Brophy's exact opposite, is a suffering, sincere socialist who
has never had the nerve to sleep with Smiles. As absorbed by his
political commitments as Brophy is by himself, Peter recites a litany of
liberal guilt:

> I want you to feel responsible.
> I want you to feel the pain of Gavin dying.
> I want you to feel involved.
> I want you to feel sorry for him.
> I want you to feel.
> Collective responsibility begins here. (110)

The death of Peter's brother, Gavin, about which the audience learns
little, hangs over the play. In scene 8 Smiles tells Brophy, "I've always
thought Gavin's murder was integral to your success. You must make
up your mind whether you killed him or not" (119–20). Brophy is not
literally directly responsible for Gavin's death. His measure of responsibility lies in the collective responsibility Peter identifies. Peter comes
to the conclusion that Brophy "killed Gavin out of sheer bravado but
this rotten penal system of ours looks like punishing you for it. . . . I
want to cure not punish" (121). The most likely explanations for
Brophy's fall from public favor are that he eventually did feel some
measure of collective responsibility that undermined his cynical detachment, or that the public simply grew accustomed to and hence bored
by him.

In contrast to Leonard and the snivelling Peter, Brophy's irreverence
toward social consciousness seems refreshing yet cold-blooded, candid
yet calloused. Admittedly self-interested and concerned only with his
own pleasures, he has no faith in social causes. As he tells Smiles, "You
still think there's something pure and positive about protest. You think
that screaming like a lunatic helps. You think that outrage changes
things. But it doesn't. Nothing changes" (108). Hardly anomalous
among Hare's characters, Brophy finds an easy target in idealism and
success in his aloofness, his coolness.

From the first words of the play, "The epic," *How Brophy Made Good*
acknowledges its use of Brechtian techniques. Its episodic structure,

narration, direct address, music, and overt theatricality all mark *Brophy* as an application of Brechtian stagecraft to the experimental, politically oriented theater of the late sixties. Satirical fantasies, like Brophy's anonymous, menacing phone calls, punctuate the play. Scene 8 fantasizes a future revolution in England with Brophy as its hero: "If there is to be a revolution. Then let it happen on colour television in front of a thousand microphones with most people just sitting but an elite commentating and the whole thing mirrored into a million homes" (115). This particular fantasy evaporates as quickly as it materializes, but not before evoking the French situationists and reinforcing the power of the media to shape as well as to report events.[3]

The satire of *How Brophy Made Good* takes aim at the media and at "the ruling class of English socialism" (123). Underlying the lighthearted barbs, however, is a genuine disillusionment with the Labour government and with the liberal cause in general that resurfaces in *The Great Exhibition* and, to a lesser extent, in *Fanshen*.

Slag

Slag is "gals" spelled backwards, but it is also British slang for a slavish toady, and especially for a woman used only as a sexual object. In *How Brophy Made Good* Brophy uses the word in the context of defending his lust for Smiles to Peter: "I don't nurse my desires. I own up to the slag I want" (99). *Slag* is the first of Hare's plays to focus on women, although here they are less important as psychologically complex individuals than as ideological mouthpieces.

Slag begins at Brackenhurst, a girls' boarding school in the provinces, as Joanne leads the entire faculty of three in the recitation of a vow to abjure men and sex: "To abstain from all forms and varieties of sexual intercourse. . . . To keep my body intact in order to register my protest against the way our society is run by men for men whose aim is the subjugation of the female and the enslavement of the working woman. . . . All forms of sex I therefore deny myself in order to work toward the establishment of a truly socialist society."[4] Although Ann and Elise barely tolerate Joanne's dogmatic schemes for creating a feminist, socialist revolution at Brackenhurst, they dutifully recite her oath. The relationships among the three women are based on their caustic wit and mutual affection and vilification. Ann tells Joanne "your opinions [are] pure balls and your mind irretrievably shallow" (35). As headmistress, Ann is necessarily concerned with retaining the fast dwindling number of pupils enrolled at their exclusive experimental public school. Ann's conventional ideas about improving the school—painting halls, building a new cricket pavillion—are dismissed by Elise as "hopeless optimism" (16).

Ann subscribes to the belief that sex, religion, and politics are not suitable subjects for discussion. Nearly as polemic as Joanne's advocacy of feminism is Ann's rejection of it: "I am a woman and I'm inferior to men. The woman's place is below, beneath and under men. . . . I will fight to the death for my right to be inferior. Inferiority is a privilege I wish to preserve. I don't want to be equal. And I don't want my girls equal. And I don't want a socialist community" (50). Ann, at thirty-two the oldest of the three, holds "old-fashioned" values and goals, none of which is shared by Elise or Joanne.

Joanne consistently undermines Ann's traditional idea of progress by, among other things, teaching students, the "Royal child" in particular, to masturbate. Joanne is at odds with the other two in her political views, schizophrenia, paranoia, self-pity, militant feminism, youth, and idealism. Setting herself apart from Ann and Elise, Joanne fancies herself an artist: "Not the kind of artist that actually has anything to do with art. It wouldn't touch it eeurch. Culture eeurch. But an artist in the way I am. I want gold cherubs blowing trumpets over my bed and an ivory bathtub to wash in" (28–29). And this comes from a woman who wants a socialist feminist revolution. Joanne's inconsistencies also appear in her contradictory ideas about Brackenhurst: she sees the school as the opportunity to create a feminist revolution, but she also "hate[s] children" (22) and is "determined to leave" (29). Ann twice fires Joanne, but also prevents her from leaving the school.

Elise supposedly conceives a child to whom she plans to devote her life. She spends her time knitting booties for her imaginary child, lamenting the fact that she did not pursue a modeling career, and arguing with Joanne. Joanne upbraids Elise for wanting a child, owning stock, sleeping with men, being a "class traitor" (45), and claiming to be normal. In return, Elise ridicules Joanne, especially for her upper-class Cheltenham background.

None of the three spends much time in the classroom. Their pedagogy consists primarily of leaving "that bossy one in charge" (14). They seem to have only contempt for the girls they supposedly teach: Ann dismisses one as a "stupid girl" (32); Joanne calls the student body "eight benighted little sods" (29); Elise refers to them as "freaks" (15). Elise and Joanne both refer to the fact that nothing changes at

Brackenhurst—nothing except the ever-declining number of students enrolled. Teaching rarely interrupts their arguments, and the audience never sees a student.

Much of the play is taken up with the animosity and hatred of these three women. Elise says that she hates Joanne (33); Joanne admits that the children hate her (34); Ann describes Joanne as "neurotic and miserable" (49). Ironically, many of the insults they hurl at each other are sexist in nature: "Sodden flabby cow" (30); "She's off her tiny tits" (19).

As they meet at the beginning of the January term, the school has lost all of its pupils as well as its direction. Elise tells Ann and Joanne, "There's nothing in our lives that's worth redeeming. . . . And while you've been talking the children have left. You've lived so long on other people's behalf you've ceased to recognize yourselves. There's nothing here worth keeping and certainly nothing holds us together" (76). Not until the very end of the play does any common ground emerge, when bound together by their failure or at least their experience, they decide to go on.

As in *The Great Exhibition,* Hare here creates characters remarkable for their self-absorption. Although they talk incessantly about social issues, political causes, and philosophical positions, they manage to accomplish virtually nothing. Joanne, like Hammett in *The Great Exhibition,* makes much of her suffering: "There are times when I feel I've suffered so much that the world has just got to move over and yield" (72). Her self-pity and paranoia, like Hammett's, are excuses for not taking actions that might result in some change or progress. And, like the characters in *The Great Exhibition,* they seem to be lurching toward entropy. Their attacks on each other, often as funny as they are vicious, belie the power of their sisterhood.

Underlying their vituperations is a struggle among the three women, principally to assert their own convictions, that anticipates the ideological struggles played out in personal terms in *Fanshen.* Hare says that *Slag* was "really a play about institutions, not about women at all. . . . It's about every institution I had known—school, Cambridge, Pathé, and so on. They are all the same. That is how institutions perpetuate themselves. With rituals that go on inside them—ever more baroque discussion about ever dwindling subjects."[5] The world these women inhabit and create is sealed off as a rejection of or escape from society. There is little in the way of love among them and even less agreement on what they are about; only the triangle of interdependence binds the three together. They end weary of each other and their experiment, yet they plan to continue—together.

Like all of Hare's satires, *Slag* relies heavily on hyperbole and fantasy. Joanne's efforts to leave Brackenhurst, for instance, include attempts to scale a high wire fence and to tunnel out from her bedroom. (Joanne, who loves films, sees this and most of her experiences in terms of a movie: "*The Great Escape,* John Sturges, 1963" [67].) The fantastic elements in *Slag* include not only the assemblage of three unlikely colleagues, but Elise's hysterical pregnancy, which Joanne would like to see as reproduction exclusively by women without the need for men. Joanne's departure, Elise's pregnancy, and Ann's dream of a model academy are all, in fact, fantasies. There is far more talk than substance to any of their plans for the future. And while the three plan and fantasize, the days slip by with nothing accomplished.

Ruby Cohn argues that *Slag* "is situationally derived from *Love's Labor's Lost.*"[6] Citing the separationist oaths that begin both plays, she writes that Hare "mocks his trio of female academics more ferociously than ever Shakespeare does his would-be monks."[7] Cohn also suggests that Hare "may well owe a debt to Sartre's *Huis clos,* as well as to Shakespeare, for the three are in hell much of the time."[8] The crucial difference is that Hare's characters, unlike Sartre's, can leave, but for their own reasons—in fear or rejection of the outside world—choose to stay.

Critics are generally ambivalent about the attitude toward women and feminism expressed in *Slag*. Some accused Hare of writing an openly misogynistic play. Hare responds that "it was written at a time when I was deeply impressed, delighted with women. It's written as a play in praise of women. I always protest when people claim that it's a misogynist play."[9]

Slag was initially produced by Michael Codron at the Hampstead Theatre Club in April 1970 and revived a year later at the Royal Court in a production with Lynn Redgrave, Anna Massey, and Barbara Ferrise. Well received in England, *Slag* won for Hare the London *Evening Standard* award as the most promising new playwright of 1970, impressive recognition only two years after his graduation from Cambridge and entrance into the theatrical world. Produced by Joseph Papp for the New York Shakespeare Festival the next year, it was also the first of his plays to reach America. Clive Barnes, in the *New York Times,* praised Hare as "dexterously talented" and described *Slag* as "a fantasy about the decline of English society—its new rootlessness—as symbolized, Ionesco-fashion, by the disintegration of the school."[10]

The relevance of an early work like *Slag* to Hare's distinctive, mature work lies in his treatment of idealism and the struggle of characters to reconcile abstract beliefs and personal actions. As in his later plays, the mundane realities these women confront belie and undermine their lofty abstract convictions. Hare would develop vastly greater subtlety and complexity, especially in his characterization of women. In *Slag*, weighed down by an inescapable class structure, dogmatism, and self-doubt, the beliefs of these three women are played out in what Hare acknowledges is an overly schematic formula.

The Great Exhibition

Hare says that "the only political experience I had had [before writing *The Great Exhibition*] was believing passionately in the Labour Government of 1964, and watching that government sell everything down the river. So the play was about a disillusioned Labour MP."[11] In 1964 Harold Wilson led to power Britain's first Labour government since Clement Atlee's (1945–51). But by the end of the 1960s the Labour government's failures had disheartened and dispirited large numbers of liberals. And by 1972 the failure, if not betrayal, of the liberal agenda—social equality, provision of basic services, equitable distribution of wealth, a classless society—was inescapable. Edward Heath, elected prime minister in 1970, ended the tenure of Wilson by gaining for the Conservatives a slim (forty-three-vote) majority over Labour. Today political scientists are virtually unanimous in their assessment of Wilson's Labour governments as ineffectual and disappointing.

Prefaced by a table charting the distribution of private property between 1911 and 1960 that shows a meager 7 percent drop in the total net private capital held by the wealthiest 10 percent of the total population, *The Great Exhibition* looks not on specific failures of the Wilson government, but on those of Charlie Hammett, a Liberal M.P. The drugs, suspicions, and infidelities that surround Hammett are as debilitating as Britain's deepening problems, the worst of which seems to be Britain's politicians. By focusing on the disintegration of Hammett's marriage, career, and stability, *The Great Exhibition* attempts to parallel personal and political disillusionment. Like *Slag*, *The Great Exhibition* is structured around triangular relationships. Here two triangles involve Charlie and Maud Hammett; Maud's Australian lover, Jerry, completes the first, but the second triangle is vastly more complicated by Catriona, Hammett's lover and Maud's friend.

Act 1, Public Life, moves through nine hours in Hammett's life. Since Hammett withdrew from public life six weeks earlier, he has become a recluse: he doesn't attend debates in Parliament, doesn't visit his constituents in Sunderland, doesn't even answer the phone. Maud, who promptly announces that she plans to leave Hammett because she no longer loves him, describes his problem as a "diminishing personality": "You remember the tribal superstition that somebody photographed has had a bit taken away. Well, that's Charlie's idea of public life. That by some incredible process he's been cannibalized."[12] His suffering, self-absorbed and self-reflexive, feeds upon itself: "I've handed out my life in small parcels and who ever gave me anything back?" (27).

Hammett hires a detective, Abel, to investigate his wife's supposed infidelities. Hiding in the cupboard, Abel has no trouble whatever in discovering Maud's affair with Jerry since it is going on in the next room. Hammett inserts Abel's Polaroid photo of Maud and Jerry in flagrante delicto in a desktop frame.

To Clough, the erstwhile Home Secretary, Hammett spews out his disgust with politics in general and the Labour party in particular: "I'm disillusioned with Parliamentary democracy. . . . Even if the system worked, which it doesn't, would it be worth it? . . . Show me one M.P. who resembles a man. Not a pedant or a hypocrite or a mental cripple or a liar or an egomaniac or a performer or a fool" (28). Hammett's disgust is not with insuperable political problems, but with those charged with solving those problems. Importantly, Hammett falls into no fewer than three of these categories himself: he is a hypocrite, an egomaniac, a performer, and quite possibly a fool.

Hammett's disillusionment also extends to his wife, whom he met in 1962 during the protest marches against nuclear armaments at Aldermaston. He rhapsodizes to Abel about their courtship in sleeping bags and about his proposal to her that "drew heavily on *Das Kapital*" (33). But whatever common ground they enjoyed during their courtship has long since vanished. Maud and Hammett argue over who is going to leave whom; finally Maud walks out, telling her husband, "Suffering is so much your undisputed territory that no one else is allowed near" (43).

In scene 3 the set of Hammett's room flies apart, transporting him to Clapham Common, a spacious public park, at 1 A.M. Saturday. Hammett has reduced himself to making contact with others only by exposing himself to women in public parks. Having set for himself a quota of nineteen flashes that evening, Hammett is stunned to discover one woman who does not flee in terror, but starts up a conversation with him and turns out to have been a guest at his wedding. Catriona reports that she has come to know many of the flashers on the common and says of them "they mostly like to talk" (50). And talk Catriona and Hammett do.

Hammett's real exposure, "the great exhibition" of the play's title, is his articulation of the anxieties that plague him:

Everything that's good in us comes from our childhood. Round about ten the rot sets in. . . . The English don't know that. They're obsessed with what happens after. Why can't they get over their adolescence? . . . Always talking about schools and colleges and dormitories . . . And my first fuck and homosexual fumblings and chronic misbehaviour on the football field. . . . It's some elaborate organized hypocrisy that every Englishman thinks his birthright, and a convenient way of henceforth pretending that he has lived some sort of life, any kind of life at all. (47–48)

Only during these revelations does Catriona mockingly call out for the police. Veteran flashee, Catriona instructs Hammett on the "passing art" (51) of flashing, eliciting a performance filled with conviction and assurance, qualities that until now Hammett sadly lacked.

Six days later Hammett, now outfitted in vest, pin-striped trousers, and "a new level of deadly confidence" (54), plans his comeback in the House of Commons. Even Abel's latest report, which turns out to be more about Hammett himself than about Maud, does not disturb him. Maud, Hammett learns, also hired Abel, the first private investigator listed in the Yellow Pages, to investigate him.

As Catriona, who has now moved in with Hammett, busies herself reading the proofs for an article on syphilis in her teen magazine, their relationship founders. The day before she slept with "a horrible man from a cosmetics company" (59) for no apparent reason. Part of Hammett's renewed vigor comes from his willingness to extricate himself from his relationship with Catriona: "Suffering—the way I suffer—is only an excuse. It's only a way of not doing things . . . [now] I'm a different man" (61).

Hammett expects another visit from Clough, but Maud and Jerry arrive first. Jerry, incoherent from drugs and alcohol, is summarily dumped in another room. Maud and Catriona finally confront one another. Best friends in their days at a Swiss boarding school, Catriona

has always loved Maud. She, too, employed Abel to look into Maud
and Hammett's marriage—and for no fewer than eight years. At first
she tells Hammett that she only wants to help, but her motives become
clearer when she reveals her love for Maud; she had even attempted
suicide to capture Maud's attention and affection. She tracked down
Hammett in Clapham Common at her father's behest to persuade him
to join the Tory party. Taunted by Maud and Hammett, Catriona
finally storms out.

Drawn together in rejecting Catriona's offers of affection and political advancement, Hammett and Maud turn to the question of Hammett's seat in Parliament. Maud has quit her job as a casting director
and intends to replace him in Parliament because "socialism has been
betrayed chiefly by skyvers and bourgeois cynics like you" (79). Clough
informs them both that it is no longer simply a question of their
deciding between them who is to hold the seat in Parliament; the seat
will now go to a union secretary. Maud and Hammett curse the "bloody
workers" (81), grow nostalgic about the weekends in Sunderland they
always loathed, and see themselves as victims of the working-class
prejudice against rootless middle-class outsiders. They end up together,
confused together, as Maud says: "I was brought up—you—didn't
bother about what you did, it was true what you were. . . . My am is
superb, my does is non-existent" (83). As ineffectual as the Wilson
government, Maud and Hammett have only their good intentions to
recommend them.

Especially in comparison with Hare's later works, the fusing of the
private and public sides of Hammett's life is awkward and obvious. But
even in his self-absorption Hammett offers an eloquent statement of his
disillusionment:

The ground I've trodden on for ten years has shifted away and I'm conscious of
talking in the air. I can't even mouth the word "revolution" any longer. It
sounds so limp and second-hand. Those of us who believed that the world
would get better have been brought up short. The thing gets worse not just
because of what happens, but because the weight of knowledge of what *ought*
to happen gets greater. As things get more impossible they also get more
obvious. As our needs get simpler, they get more unlikely to be fulfilled. (52)

Not only Hammett's suffering, but Hare's wit and comic stage business link *The Great Exhibition* with *Slag*. "To me," Hare says, "a
cultivated seriousness is only so much phoney suffering. *The Great*

Exhibition is about people who suffer with a capital S—that area of self-ignorance."[13] In several of Hare's subsequent works, notably *Teeth 'n' Smiles* and *Plenty*, characters confound self-ignorance and suffering. Here, as in *Slag*, the characters' self-absorption leads them to drugs, to talk, to rivalries both real and imagined, but mainly to inaction, to entropy.

Like *Slag*, *The Great Exhibition* was first staged at the Hampstead Theatre Club and produced by Michael Codron. The production, directed by Hare, featured David Warner as Hammett and Penelope Wilton as Maud. The play, which is probably the only one to even hint at an autobiographical dimension (Hammett's wife, for instance, is a theater casting director as was Hare's), received generally mixed or poor reviews. Mary Holland was typical in her complaint that "the characters and their situation get lost so that instead of being real people they turn before our eyes into glove puppets making trendy jokes and acting out fashionable fantasies."[14]

Summation

These early plays explore diverse but distinctively British middle-class characters and settings. All are topical and, like *Lay By* and *England's Ireland*, set in the present day. All are overtly comic plays. In his later works, Hare's humor becomes much darker and more subdued. With the possible exception of Brophy before his making good, Hare's early characters fit Maud's description of herself and Hammett in *The Great Exhibition:* "We are rich, we are white, we are middle-class, we are English. We are the single most over-privileged group of people in the world" (80). These characters are also young—in their twenties—yet the choice between dedication to something outside themselves and their own self-interest is already upon them.

In 1972 Hare said, "I'm fascinated by self-enclosed societies—a very middle-class obsession."[15] Indeed, each of these early works presents a closed world as a microcosm: one that gravitates around the BBC Broadcast House in *Brophy;* the insular world of a public girls' school in provincial England in *Slag;* the confines of Hammett's shrinking world in *The Great Exhibition*. The isolation of the characters gives rise to seemingly endless talk, Brophy's stock in trade, usually to the exclusion of action. One measure of the idealism in Hare's early characters is their willingness to argue. But these very early characters' humor and openness, even if contentious, will vanish in subsequent works as characters in works like *Knuckle* and *Plenty* grow increasingly reticent—unable or unwilling to express themselves directly.

Like virtually all of Hare's plays, these early works trace the decline of characters—of their careers, their relationships, and, most important, their idealism. Convinced that the world around them is capable of and in the midst of great change, their idealism ends with the struggle to deal with disillusionment. In each instance, characters who profess a commitment to social and political causes are stymied into withdrawal or solipsism. In their closed worlds, characters become detached from social and political realities that once provided their self-definition and mission. Without a sense of identity, characters lapse into self-absorption and disillusionment.

In *Slag* and *The Great Exhibition,* at least one important difference between Hare and his compatriots in "the wild bunch" is quite evident. Hare writes not about society's criminals, but about its middle class. Rather than attack the power brokers or probe the criminals of society, Hare focuses on those who share his hopes about progress through socialism.

In a 1975 interview Hare said that, with the exception of *Knuckle* and *Teeth 'n' Smiles,* he was "happy to consign [what he had written] to oblivion."[16] Yet these plays constitute a telling apprenticeship, indicative of the themes, character types, and styles that appear in his later works.

Chapter Three
Collaborations and Adaptation

Nineteen sixty-eight, the year that Hare entered the theater world, marked the abolition of the post of Lord Chamberlain in Britain. With the barrier of censorship lifted, playwrights could address previously forbidden subjects in an explicit and often graphically violent fashion. In spite of the Lord Chamberlain's existence, the Royal Shakespeare Company produced its season of cruelty in 1964, and Edward Bond's *Saved,* denied a license by the Lord Chamberlain, appeared at the Royal Court in a private performance for members of the English Stage Society in 1965. A dozen years after Tynan called for a new, more vital and robust theater in Britain and after Osborne's Jimmy Porter appeared in *Look Back in Anger,* the impetus to shock audiences was still strong.

The dramaturgy of Hare's collaborations and one adaptation owes largely to the needs of the companies for which they were written. "Deathshead," an unpublished two-minute play, was written because the Traverse Theatre Company wanted a Christmas play to perform at the Edinburgh Festival in 1972.[1] Using double and triple casting, *Lay By* requires a cast of only six actors and very little in set design. *Brassneck,* on the other hand, written to coincide with Richard Eyre's appointment as director of the Nottingham Playhouse, is a huge play that employs dozens of characters in an epic view of three generations of the Bagley family. *Fanshen,* developed at the request of William Gaskill and Max Stafford-Clark for performance by the Joint Stock Theatre Group, requires a company of only nine actors and minimal sets. These works are shaped not only by the resources of the companies for which they were written, but also by collaboration and topicality. The violence, grotesque action, and inflammatory language of several of these collaborations are more indicative of the times in which and the companies for which they were written than of Hare's subsequent works.

Lay By

Hare offers this account of the unlikely genesis of *Lay By:*

Lay By came out of a writers' conference where, having discussed all day what was wrong with the situation of writers, I suggested that anyone who wanted should try writing a play collectively. . . . we went off and wrote, seven of us together, based on a clipping that appeared in the paper that day and which Trevor Griffiths happened to have—an extremely prurient description of an alleged rape on a motorway, and the trial. We started work the following Wednesday with wallpaper and crayons. An experiment in public writing.[2]

Collectively Hare, Howard Brenton, Brian Clark, Trevor Griffiths, Stephen Poliakoff, Hugh Stoddard, and Snoo Wilson produced a play calculated to outrage public sensibilities with its lurid subject and hyperbolic violence.

Lay By begins with a pornographer photographing Lesley and Joy while Lesley chronicles the past week by recalling the drugs and food she has ingested. The pornographer explains his business by circulating samples of his hardcore photographs to the audience.

One evening Lesley, who works at a menial job and lives with her mother, hitches a ride in a van with a couple, Marge and Jack. In a roadside lay by (i.e., rest area), Jack and a willing Lesley engage in various sexual activities while Marge sits in the van's front seat. When Jack strikes Lesley with a dog whip she objects and he stops. Lesley later explains to her friend Maureen that she has trouble recalling exactly what happened because she was taking amphetamines at the time.

When Lesley's mother sees her bruises, she contacts the police who undertake an investigation to determine if Jack and Marge "constrained [Lesley] to perform the act of fellatio."[3] In court the events are graphically reenacted with a dildo. Jack and Marge are convicted and sentenced to eight and three years, respectively.

Some time later Lesley's corpse arrives at a hospital where a doctor describes her physical condition: "Bladder distended. Colonic obstruction an informed guess. Some evidence of healed pudendic eruption. Active boils labia major. Yes. Some pururient [sic] vaginal discharge. Yes. Thighs. Further patches of perforation marks" (73). As horrific as this clinical description is, the most grotesque episode is saved for last as the attendants wash her body in blood, dump it and the bodies of Jack and Marge into an enormous bin, and cannibalize them. It is difficult to imagine a theatergoer in 1972, or at anytime, who would not have been shocked, horrified, and offended by *Lay By*. But such was precisely the intention of the playwrights. As Hare says: "I think there's something totally distinctive about the play. . . . It has got the authentic stink of pornography."[4]

The character of Lesley anticipates the utter desolation and anomie, especially chilling in a person so young, of characters in *Teeth 'n' Smiles*. Bored by her menial job, frustrated because she sees not the faintest glimmer of hope in life, she drifts into drugs, casual sex, and pornography as easily as she hitches a ride. Similar characters to appear in Hare's work, especially in *Wetherby*, are less hyperbolic, but perhaps more horrific because they are more credible.

Hare's faith in such collective exercises continued with *England's Ireland*, also produced in 1971–72, coauthored by Hare, Tony Bicât, Brian Clark, David Edgar, Francis Fuchs, Howard Brenton, and Snoo Wilson. The play was performed in Amsterdam and later in London, Glasgow, Lancaster, and Nottingham, but was effectively banned in London for "fear of being blown up."[5] Again, the collaboration focused on a topical event—the conflict in Northern Ireland. Hare's comments on this unpublished collaboration downplay its inflammatory nature: "[In a collaborative effort you] stop short at the lowest common denominator which in this case seemed to be along the lines that the fighting in Northern Ireland was blatantly the result of a colonial situation, that the English stance of neutral intervention was a farce, and that the army should withdraw as quickly as possible."[6] If nothing else, these early collaborative efforts provide one measure of Hare's idealism in the late 1960s and early 1970s. The abrasive, incendiary quality of works like *Lay By* and *England's Ireland* is by no means typical of Hare's works, but their topicality and political consciousness clearly are.

Brassneck

Written in collaboration with Brenton, *Brassneck* begins on 8 May 1945, VE-day, as Alfred Bagley hitchhikes into the fictional Midlands town of Stanton. Alfred presents himself as a man returning to his supposed hometown after having lost his wife and two shops in the Blitz. His Midlands accent, however, is as phony as his tale of woe. Bagley's first concern is to buy up as much property—preferably slum property—as he can. And the first concern of Stanton's leading businessmen is the latest turn in the "class war,"[7] the 1945 Labour party victory. Stanton's leading estate agent, James Avon, makes it clear that membership in the Masons is essential for business success and coaxes Alfred into applying for membership.

Once Alfred is inducted into the Masons, the reason behind Avon's sponsorship of him is clear: the master is quite old, and Alfred will provide another vote for Avon to become new master. As in the Masons, in local politics Avon and his cronies are opposed by Tom Browne, a Labour party member and post office employee. Deadlocked in their bids to become master in the Masons, Browne and Avon compromise on Bagley, an "utter nonentity. Worse than wallpaper" (31). In scene 5 Alfred is elected the new master and appears invested as Pope Callistus III.

Realizing that he will someday need a successor, Alfred summons his nephew Roderick. With his wife, Vanessa, and three children, Sidney, Martin, and Lucy, Roderick arrives in Stanton hoping for a brief deathbed visit and a handsome inheritance. But Alfred intends to set up Roderick as an architect to build an empire. Against the background of postwar food rationing, Alfred explains to James Avon his new way of doing business: "We all put our tenders in. But first everyone reveals them to me. I reveal them to Roderick. Who puts in last. And lowest. And wins" (42–43). Should Avon balk at this arrangement, Alfred is prepared to publicize the X-rays of Avon's son's supposed war injuries, "Wounds compatible with a Boy Scout knife" (43). Avon sees no choice but to accept Alfred's offer.

In the final scene of act 1 Alfred arranges for the marriage of Roderick's daughter Lucy to coincide with the coronation of Queen Elizabeth. By now the family's depravity appears almost congenital. Alfred's patriarchal tribute to his niece runs amok. Instead of delivering the customary platitudes, he drifts into the truth by describing what prepared him for a career in commercial exploitation, his experiences in the trenches during World War I: "I saw a man eating . . . you know, human flesh . . . Long pork, we called it . . . What were tasty were human brain . . . if rats didn't get there before we English Tommies. Funny, having to go to war t'see inside o' human brain for first time" (55). As the festivities progress with a tap dancer, Alfred seizes an oversized knife, slams it on the table, screams the Masonic password, "BOAZ" (58), and collapses in death.

Act 2 moves forward to the late 1960s. Lucy, now thirty-five, has been through three husbands; Roderick, master of the Stanton Vale hunt, has acquired all the affectations of the landed gentry; Vanessa has drifted into lunatic poetry; and Sidney, their son, has succeeded his great-uncle Alfred as the principal deal-maker of the family business. The burghers of Stanton, with the exception of Clive Avon, have fallen into their proper ranks in the Bagley empire. Harry Edmunds complains of being hoodwinked out of a junket to Hong Kong, but his dissent is nothing more than sarcasm: "It's all been a Bagley mystery tour," says Edmunds. "We're all on this bus. Tickets taken away. Door locked" (71). While Roderick is off to the hounds, the Bagley faithful gather to meet Raymond Finch, whom Clive describes as "Tory ex-Minister. Longtime Junior in Colonial Office. Sometime Senior in Ministry of Housing. When out of office will offer Governmental expertise on Private Industry. . . . A respectable man, respected, a blazer for other men to wear. Ministers available, cut out the form at the back of the investor's chronicle. Vaseline man" (75–76). But even after Clive covers Finch with horse manure, figuratively and then literally, he grovels his apologies and then accepts his punishment. The drainage deal in Cardiff promised to Clive is canceled. After Finch slinks off to clean himself up, the doom of the Bagley empire is sealed when Martin announces Roderick's bankruptcy.

The bankruptcy proceedings uncover an array of irregularities that bring Roderick to trial for fraud. Under Tom Browne's influence, the Labour Club offers Roderick its facilities during his trial. Browne has to explain what has happened to Roderick, who remains oblivious to his own corruption. "You admitted you gave a bribe. . . . It was everything. It was graft. It was corruption. It was Chicago. When you said 'Gift' everyone in that court looked at you. And suddenly . . . You were a spiv. Because this morning you were a bankrupt. But tonight you're a fraud" (89).

Brassneck ends years later on the day of Roderick's release from prison in 1973 in Sidney's sleazy strip joint, The Lower Depths Club. There the old Bagley retainers once again convene. Edmunds complains of having to sit across from Finch "and all the other refugees from scandal and debauch" (97) in the House of Lords. Clive has become the new Mr. Lucy. Martin has become a "Eurocrat" in Brussels, well respected and using his Christian name as his surname. To this company in his seedy bôite, Sidney announces his plan to resurrect the Bagley empire by dealing in Chinese heroin.

Characters   Alfred Bagley is a "man who believes in nothing" (55) largely as a consequence of his experience in World War I. Like all of Hare's characters, Alfred exists in a historical context—inescapably and inevitably, he is shaped by events larger than himself. As in all of Hare's plays, experience cannot be cordoned off into discrete areas of war, business, and domesticity. The connection between what Alfred experienced during World War I and what he becomes after World War II is not casual but causal. Cannibalism in the trenches prepared him for the dog-eat-dog world of business.

Although few of these characters are complex, there is an important distinction between Alfred and his nephew Roderick. Alfred's experience during World War I is indisputably the key to his Darwinian view of life. He realizes that hypocrisy is the surest way of gaining success and acceptance among the power brokers of Stanton. Alfred observes the pieties of family and nation, no matter how insincerely. Although he hated his wife, killed her in fact, Alfred pretends that he suffers because of her death. When he first approaches Avon about acquiring property in Stanton, he couches his request in the platitudes of respectability.

Roderick does not share his uncle's horrific wartime experiences but readily accepts Alfred's corruption without conscience. He buys into the Bagley dream with complete amorality—devoid of any sense of the consequences or repercussions of exploitation. Similarly, Martin, whose meticulous records finally undo the Bagley family, is oblivious to the implications of his "family history" (91). Only Sidney clearly sees what Alfred realized about the world of business. Recalling *How Brophy Made Good* in its treatment of public relations and the media, Sidney explains: "Three-quarters of the business is public relations . . . fixing contracts, arranging tenders, that sort of thing. A kind of banking. Human banking. Building up a pool of friends to be cashed at any branch" (82). Moreover, the character of Tom Browne, first a humble post office worker and the Labour party outcast, later the right worshipful mayor of Stanton, and finally the sycophantic public relations manager of the Bagley empire, recalls Hammett in *The Great Exhibition*. Both are characters who subscribe to the liberal/Labour cause, but find that their convictions are not nearly as strong as the lure of complacency.

There is very little to admire in these characters. Corruption is limited neither to the Bagleys nor to the old boy network: a former Tory minister, a Labour M. P., a solicitor, and a European diplomat all partake of it. The best among them, Clive Avon, fakes a war injury that later enables Alfred to blackmail Clive's father. Clive's finest moment comes when he covers Finch with horse manure, but he then abjectly apologizes for what he has done. Finch ends in the House of Lords while Clive remains merely a feckless pest to the Bagleys.

What happens to the women in this play is especially chilling. As Vanessa more fully appreciates what her ambitions for Roderick have led to, she composes lyrics to the Midland depravity. Late in the play,

Roderick toys with the idea of salvaging his empire by having Vanessa certified as insane so that he can take control of the companies in her name (a scheme Malloy will employ in *Knuckle*). But their daughter Lucy is perhaps the most ruthless of them all. From her first appearance as a spoiled brat at the age of fourteen to her drunken vulgarity at her first wedding, she changes little. Married four times and divorced three, she is as joyless as she is self-centered.

Themes and Imagery   *Brassneck* depicts capitalism in terms of human brokerage. People are commodities, bought and sold like pork bellies, real estate, or drugs. The deals that fuel society are blackmail, extortion, graft, and bribery. And the traditions and hierarchies of society only assure a continuity from one generation of corruption to the next. Like Shaw and Brecht, Hare and Brenton portray capitalistic society as a brothel. Clive characterizes the Bagleys "as brothelkeepers" (82). Alfred himself jokingly uses the image to describe his status as slum landlord: "I don't want to run the brothel, son. I just want the girls" (44).

The image of Alfred as Callistus III explicitly points to the Bagleys' allegorical relationship to the fifteenth-century Borgias. Like the Bagleys, the Borgias were outsiders transplanted to the scene of their empire building. Since Cardinal Alfons Borgia was elected Pope Callistus III in 1445, *Brassneck* marks the five-hundred-year anniversary of the ascent of the Borgias. Like Alfred Bagley when he is elected Masonic master, Alfons Borgia was a compromise candidate when he was elected pope. As one chronicler of the Borgias describes him, Alfons was "a man to whom no one could object,"[8] someone who was unlikely to live very long. In 1456 Callistus invested his nephew, Rodrigo Borgia (Roderick's counterpart) in the College of Cardinals. The beneficiary of nepotism who also holds the distinction of being the first to buy his election to the papacy, Rodrigo became Pope Alexander VI in 1492. Rodrigo's mistress, Vannozza Catanei, bore him three children, Cesare (Sidney), Giovanni (Martin), and the infamous Lucrezia (Lucy) Borgia. But not even the Borgias rival the Bagleys in wickedness. Machiavelli idealized Cesare Borgia in *The Prince*. Modern historians regard Lucrezia as an "innocent victim"[9] of her father and brothers. Virtually devoid of any positive human qualities, the Bagleys are cartoons of capitalistic evil who evoke the popular misapprehension of the Borgias' consummate depravity in their simony, nepotism, congenital evil, and ruthless exploitation. Its title slang for criminal nerve,

Brassneck evoked for the British audiences in the mid-1970s the Poulson scandal that exposed an intricate network of price-fixing schemes and corruptions that centered on the largest architectural firm in Europe, owned by John Poulson, an unlicensed architect.

Pravda

The second collaboration between Hare and Brenton, *Pravda* is remarkably similar in spirit and theme, although unambiguously a comedy. The most commercially successful of Hare's plays, it is the second longest-running production ever presented at Britain's National Theatre. Although written eleven years after *Brassneck, Pravda* can be reasonably grouped with the earlier collaboration with Brenton because of its depiction of capitalism. Both plays, moreover, depend upon grotesque characters, farcical action, and didactic lessons more typical of Hare's collaborations than his own works.

The play's principal character, Lambert La Roux, originally played by Anthony Hopkins, is loosely modeled on the Australian media tycoon Rupert Murdoch. An utterly unscrupulous entrepreneur whose only virtues are his consistency and candor, La Roux is an unprincipled businessman, an acquisitive capitalist, and a bully. His past in South Africa is shady, and his humanity dubious. Like Alfred Bagley and Sarrafian in *Teeth 'n' Smiles,* La Roux sees life as the survival of the fittest; beyond the material, he holds no values whatever.

Opposing La Roux is Andrew May, a boyish Everyman who rises to the rank of editor, first at a provincial newspaper and later at a "British institution"[10] that roughly approximates the London *Times.* May's rise and fall, dependent on La Roux's whims, is as precipitous as that of the Bagleys. Initially, May is an innocent. Attracted by his idealism, his wife, Rebecca, brings a crusading optimism to May's journalistic ambitions. Rebecca confidently gives her husband a stolen government document on the public health danger in transporting radioactive substances. She believes that May and his staff will welcome the opportunity to expose the hazard and to shame the government with the truth. May realizes that publishing the report in La Roux's newspaper will mean the end of his career. With Rebecca, May defects to a rival paper which publishes the document. They, however, are still fired and then prosecuted for violating government security regulations.

The crisis of the play focuses on May's defiance of La Roux. Through his toady, Sylvester, La Roux tricks May into believing a phony episode from the past would compromise La Roux's public image. After May publishes the damning story in his alternative newspaper, *The Usurper,* La Roux tracks him down on the Yorkshire Moors. La Roux is out killing birds; May, yet another of La Roux's prey, is out hiking. Faced with La Roux's threat of a lawsuit for libel, May accepts defeat and goes back to work for La Roux.

Pravda is a hyperbolic morality play in which good—represented by Rebecca—contends with and loses to evil—epitomized by La Roux—for the soul of Andrew May. This contemporary morality play demonstrates that goodness is not assured victory: May is trapped as the foreman in La Roux's "foundry of lies" at the end of a play whose title means "Truth."

In an interview Hare stated that he and Brenton "both dreamt of the kind of play we enjoy seeing when we go to the theatre—big plays, full of characters and incident, comedies, taking on large subjects—and we willed one into existence."[11] Like *Brassneck, Pravda* is indeed a big play—sprawling, full of characters, larger than life, but it offers neither the subtlety of characterization nor the complexity of emotion that distinguishes Hare's own works. Minor characters, with names like Ian Ape-Warden or Elliot Fruit-Norton, are as numerous as they are exaggerated. Hare's collaborations with Brenton create worlds that are cartoons of capitalistic evil in which characters are grotesque caricatures and events depend upon bizarre coincidences. The comic and satiric impulse here is much stronger than in his own plays largely because many of the characters are straw men.

Fanshen

With the bankruptcy of the Portable Theatre, Hare founded another theater company in 1973, this time in conjunction with David Aukin and Max Stafford-Clark. In August 1974 the Joint Stock Theatre Group undertook the collaborative adaptation of William Hinton's *Fanshen,* an account of land reform in a Chinese village. Over the next year, a series of workshops, revisions, and collaborative rehearsals produced Hare's *Fanshen.*

The evolution of *Fanshen* suggests not only Hare's faith in drama as a political instrument but also his continuing faith in the collaborative process. When William Gaskill and Stafford-Clark originally proposed Hinton's book as the basis for a Joint Stock production, the subject of the book itself suggested the collaborative process which took the form of workshops. In his memoir on the Joint Stock Company Hare assesses the relative roles of actors, directors, and playwrights in these workshops: "I worked on trying to digest and master the extraordinary complexity of the book, while, in workshop, the actors flung themselves at whatever bit they fancied, more or less in whatever style they fancied. The writer represented reason, the actors imagination."[12] Hare wrote "a text that was as resonant of Europe as was possible, so that people might make their own analogies, about political leadership and so on."[13] Since the play's original audiences were British, this shift seems completely natural. Moreover, the idea of self-criticism that figures so importantly in Hinton's book and Hare's play was integral to the workshops.

Gaskill's involvement in directing Brecht's works in England and the subject matter of Hinton's book virtually assured the application of political dialectic in *Fanshen*. For Gaskill, *Fanshen* was "a fulfillment of the process . . . in which actors share an understanding of the political responsibility of the play; they are not just there to serve the writer but, together with the writer, are making a statement."[14] The Brechtian influence is obvious in the episodic and epic structure, the use of slogans, and the emphasis on man as a social rather than a psychological creature. The actors first enter and address the audience with statistics about the village of Long Bow and its inhabitants. Instead of psychological complexity, the emphasis falls on observation of the class structure, Long Bow's redistribution of limited wealth, and the idealistic effort to purge self-interest.

Fanshen literally means "to turn the body" or "to turn over"—as in the turning over from feudalism to Communism that took place in China in the late 1940s. Metaphorically, *fanshen* suggests a cleansing and a politicization of society. In Hare's own words: "To China's hundreds of millions of landless and land-poor peasants it meant to stand up, to throw off the landlord yoke, to gain land, stock, implements, and houses. . . . It meant to enter a new world."[15]

Set between 1945 and 1949, *Fanshen* dramatizes Long Bow's effort to achieve justice through equitable sharing among its citizens. T'ien-Ming, the Communist party representative, invites the peasants of Long Bow to accuse their oppressors by specifying the injustices they have personally endured. Because the peasants have little knowledge of the alternatives to the feudal system under which they have always lived, Secretary Liu attempts to educate them about the structure of their society by explaining that although the peasants depend upon the land and landowners to earn their livings, the landowners depend upon the peasants to grow and to harvest the crops. The accusations, arraignments, and torture of the landlords continue; some confess to hoarding the money and grain they have exacted from the peasants. The wealth of the fifteen wealthiest families is redistributed; need, and the degree to which peasants have spoken out against their oppressors, determine their shares. The citizens are divided into three groups: landlords, middle peasants, and poor peasants. The poorest have the first opportunity to take what they need; afterwards, the leaders of the movement receive less.

After several wrenching and brutal attempts to equalize the limited resources of Long Bow, the Communist party decrees that the peasants must be mobilized in the war effort and now orders that the property of the middle peasants must be redistributed. This time citizens will be evaluated not only on the basis of their own needs, but in light of their father's and grandfather's deeds, specifically whether their ancestors exploited the peasants at any time in the past. This evaluation leads to more torture in the effort to uncover more hoarded wealth.

After T'ien-Ming leaves his wife and four-year-old daughter to work at the Communist party's County Headquarters, a party work team arrives. One of them is attacked by the vice chairman of the Peasant Association. In response, the work team suspends the authority of all community organizations—Women's Association, the militia, the peasant groups. Hou, the work-team leader, concludes, "The place is rotten. We must start again" (39). Revised plans for redistribution set still different criteria based only on need and the classification of the population as poor peasants, middle peasants, and rich peasants, or landlords. To that end, two of the cadres must face "the Gate," an ordeal in which they must criticize themselves by acknowledging their faults and failures before the community. One of them, Cheng K'uan, fails the Gate because of self-interest; the other, Hseuh-Chen, passes the Gate, submits to the people, and accepts the unlikely suggestion that she change the way she looks.

When the party work team returns to Lucheng County Headquarters Hou reports on the situation in Long Bow. Secretary Ch'en summarily judges the work team's efforts in Long Bow an example of "Left deviation": "You have sought support only from poor peasants, thereby neglecting the middle peasants. You've treated Party members as if they were class enemies" (56–57). When Hou conveys this criticism to the work team, the process of self-criticism now turns to Hou and the lack of leadership he has provided.

The work team returns to Long Bow, but there is no wealth left to be redistributed, only poverty. No one is interested in yet another meeting for classification, until Hsien-E decides to give evidence against two party members: her father-in-law, Yu-lai, and her husband, Wen-te. Fearing reprisals, Hsien-E agrees to testify only on the condition that she can divorce her husband, an unprecedented event in Long Bow. The charges against Yu-lai and Wen-te steadily mount. Hou announces: "This case demands . . . the severest punishment. Party members have a trust which you have betrayed. The people say you must go to the County Court" (69). Yu-Lai's alternatives are to admit and assess his failures or to despair and face death. The cadres decide that Yu-Lai can neither be allowed to despair nor simply be punished. He must be re-educated because, as Liu says, "There are no breakthroughs in our work. There is no 'just do this one thing and we will be there.' There is only the patient, daily work of re-making people. Over each hill, another hill. Over that hill, a mountain. The Party needs Yu-Lai because he is clever and strong, and reformed will be of more value to the people than if he had never been corrupted. We must save him. We can use him. He can be reformed" (72). The action of the play moves through such an unending succession of redistributions and purges. In each, the criteria for who will be punished or rewarded change. The goal to set aside self-interest and personal ambition can be reached only by revising the way in which individuals see themselves in relation to their community. As Hare says, in "a post-revolutionary society, like China . . . the dialectic is actually seen to mean something in people's lives. In the play *Fanshen* it is dynamic. Political practice answers to political theory and yet modifies it; the party answers to the people and is modified by it. The fight is for political structures which answer people's needs; and people themselves are changed by living out theoretical ideas."[16]

Although set twenty-five years earlier and in an entirely different culture, *Fanshen* examines a political ideal worked out on distinctly human terms. The characters here are difficult to pin down because the criteria by which they are judged and judge themselves often shift. But, like all of Hare's work, *Fanshen* is not the abstract incarnation of an ideology; its ideals are constantly shaped and qualified by human realities. Despite the systematic effort to reassess the individual's rela-tionship to the community, human foibles remain. Two comic instances, the demand that Hseuh-Chen change her looks and Hsien-E's insistence on divorce, both grow out of self-interest and human nature.

There are other important connections with Hare's concerns of this period. He does not set up straw men in the enemies of socialism but, as in earlier plays, examines the dilemmas of those already committed to that cause. And as always, politics exist in human contexts. *Fanshen* is an excellent example of a political play that not only accommodates both the individual and the ideological, the personal and the public, but also avoids what Hare sees as the "appalling overkill"[17] of much political theater in Britain in the 1970s. In his 1978 lecture at King's College, Cambridge, Hare lamented that Brecht and the Marxist playwrights in general indulge "the godlike feeling that the questions have been answered before the play has begun."[18] Hare's alternative lies first, in fusing the personal and the political; second, in refusing to presume that an ideology is a panacea; and third, in humor. At the play's end, the process of reform continues as yet another meeting is convened to the peasants' obvious disdain.

Hare believes that this was unquestionably a period in Chinese history when the lives of ordinary people were measurably improved by a process that, while painful, was absolutely essential to the betterment of the community. Hare also acknowledges that the members of the Joint Stock Theatre Group were conscious of applying the observations in Hinton's book to make *Fanshen* accessible to Western audiences. Infused by a communal and nonhierarchial spirit, the production of *Fanshen* and the evolution of its dramatic text owes much to the idealism of Hare, his directors, and the company.

Like the Portable Theatre, these workshops took on a kind of celebrity—partially for their success, partially because of the risks involved. The workshop format itself is still in modified use by Stafford-Clark and Caryl Churchill. (Their most recent and most successful collaborative venture is *Serious Money.*) Hare's recent assessment of *Fanshen* is that "an openly political way of working only pays off with dialectical material"[19] such as Hinton's book.

Fanshen was first performed in Sheffield in April 1975 and later that same month in London at the Institute for Contemporary Arts (ICA) Terrace Theatre. Several of the London reviews of *Fanshen* admired the ensemble playing and the distinctly human approach to a highly political subject. Calling *Fanshen* a "beautifully written play . . . a moving and impressively lucid account," Michael Coveney praised its "exuberant optimism"[20] and humor.

Summation

In style, theme, and characterization, the collaborations and the adaptation are more indicative of the Fringe in the late 1960s and early 1970s than are the earliest of his solely authored works. Not only are these plays more overtly political in subject and more Brechtian in dramaturgy, but—with the exception of *Pravda*—they are devoid of the romance and personal idealism characteristic of Hare's own works. Abrasive, hyperbolic, and polemic, the collaborations and the adaptation indicate the path that Hare could have but did not follow as his reaction against overtly didactic writing took root. The biting humor, often savage and grotesque, does not reappear until *Pravda* and, to a far lesser extent, *Wrecked Eggs*.

In 1974 Howard Brenton judged that "the fringe has failed. Its failure was that of the whole dream of an 'alternative culture'—the notion that within society as it exists you can grow another way of life, which, like a beneficent and desirable cancer, will in the end grow throughout the western world, and change it. What happens is that the 'alternative society' gets hermetically sealed, and surrounded. A ghetto-like mentality develops. It is surrounded, and, in the end, strangled to death."[21] Indeed, after the mid-1970s, Hare and several of his Fringe colleagues made a deliberate effort to move into established theaters and to seek out different audiences. Beginning with *Knuckle*, Hare's plays would reach wider and more commercial audiences not only because they were less polemic and more literary but because his distinctive voice addressed experiences common to people who were neither intellectuals nor revolutionaries. Among Hare's works since 1975, *Pravda* remains anomalous not only for its collaborative origin but for its hyperbole.

Chapter Four
Knuckle and *Teeth 'n' Smiles*

In his 1978 lecture at King's College, Cambridge, Hare lamented that British theater in the mid-1970s was dominated by plays from three categories: those employing "political overkill"; those expressing comfortable West End "reassurances"; and "upper middle-brow, intellectual comedies."[1] Making his own way through this theatrical minefield, Hare turned to distinctly British contemporary subjects in the 1970s, ones that were "simply ignored, or appropriated for the shallowest purposes: rock music, black propaganda, gun-selling, diplomacy."[2] The broad, slapstick humor of earlier plays now yields to a stylized wit and an often bitter irony in the language of these plays.

As in his collaborations with Brenton, *Knuckle* and *Teeth 'n' Smiles* depict capitalism as a disease spread by carriers and infecting virtually everyone. But in these plays Hare focuses on how worlds infested with greed and corruption shape and often distort individuals. What links worlds as disparate as those of *Knuckle* and *Teeth 'n' Smiles* is not only human exploitation, but also the loss of idealism that is concomitant with the destruction of love.

Knuckle

Inspired by Ross Macdonald's thrillers, the labyrinth plot of *Knuckle* exposes the disturbing realities beneath the respectable surfaces of suburban life. David Geherin's comment on Lew Archer is immediately applicable to *Knuckle*'s protagonist, Curly Delafield. "As Archer makes his way through the well-trimmed suburbs filled with affluent people, he exposes the tragedies and fears, the sadness and failures that are the stuff of human suffering everywhere."[3] What Curly discovers about his hometown, his family, and himself is the pervasive corruption and deception that appears in many of Macdonald's novels.

The various locales of *Knuckle* defy all preconceived ideas of the Home Counties. Guildford, a comfortable suburban refuge for London's businessmen, is described as a wasteland, "a bomb site."[4] Eastbourne in Sussex, where Curly's sister was last seen, is in *Knuckle* best remembered for a gruesome murder that took place on its beach, called the Crumbles, some fifty years earlier. As Harold Hobson notes, in *Knuckle* "Eastbourne and Guildford are not peaceful, pleasant towns: out of the darkness [Hare] sees them as visions of only too imaginable horror."[5]

After a twelve-year absence from England, Curly returns to Guildford apparently because of the disappearance and presumed death of his younger sister, Sarah. Guildford, like its inhabitants, is in decay. Sarah "used to say she had contracted one of Surrey's contagious diseases— moral gumrot, internal decay" (30). "Young women in Guildford must expect to be threatened" (66), says her best friend, Jenny, which is to say that young women everywhere must expect to be threatened. Curly's reaction to his hometown is not unlike Sarah's. He left to escape cozy suburbia and their father, Patrick, "Lord Earthly-bloody Perfection" (47). Whereas Patrick, a widower, pursues a career in the City and is ostensibly respectable, right down to his pin-striped business suit and bowler hat, Curly seeks out the most disreputable trade— gunrunning—the "noisiest profession [he] could find" (51).

When Sarah disappeared from the notorious Eastbourne beach, she left behind her purse containing two first-class tickets to Victoria station; these tickets are the only direct clue about her disappearance and one that Sarah deliberately left. Having left home when Sarah was only eight years old and in the absence of any material evidence, Curly believes that his best prospect for solving the mystery of her disappearance is to find out what kind of person she was. Curly's investigation takes him first to the Shadow of the Moon Club, now owned by Jenny. Jenny describes Sarah as paranoid, constantly in need of reassurance and justification. Sarah had become involved with the previous owner of this club, Malloy—a man her own father's age who has just committed suicide and has left the club to Jenny.

Curly is extremely uneasy about returning to his father's home, where he finds Grace Dunning managing the housekeeping. The reunion between the father, who prides himself on his culture and refinement, and his gunrunning son quickly degenerates into a confrontation. Curly's attitude toward his home has changed little; as he tells his father, "This place is like silver paper between your teeth" (33).

Curly next meets Max Dupree, an investigative reporter and Sarah's one-time boyfriend, at a psychiatric institute where Jenny worked as a nurse and where Malloy's mother is a patient. Curly wonders why his father and Dupree, a "lazy, promiscuous, self-righteous bolshevik" (40), seem to be on such good terms.

When Curly returns to Patrick they discuss Sarah's moving out and disappearance. What Patrick truly resents about Sarah's earlier flight was neither that his daughter ran away from him nor that she stole £250, but that her departure was "rude and messy and—loud" (45)—precisely the indecorous behavior Patrick finds most objectionable, especially in his own children. This meeting, too, degenerates quickly: Curly accuses Patrick of a "genius for mislaying your children" (47); Patrick ridicules Curly's brash and indiscreet behavior—"peg-legging along screaming your head off fifteen paces behind the local police" (47).

At the Shadow of the Moon Club, Jenny asks Curly to take her to the beach where Sarah was last seen. Curly stops back at Patrick's to discover Mrs. Dunning in her underwear and his father in his socks and trousers. For the first time Curly glimpses some weakness, some sign of humanity in his father—a discovery that mortifies Patrick. Curly and Jenny then go off to Eastbourne—to the Crumbles, the infamous beach where the gruesome murder, the result of a failed "love experiment," took place some fifty years earlier. There Jenny glimpses the first sign of compromise in Curly when she realizes that his return to England was not motivated solely by the desire to investigate Sarah's disappearance.

Curly returns to Dupree, who has just come from Malloy's funeral. Dupree offers a ludicrous alibi for his whereabouts the night Sarah disappeared: he says he was with Patrick and a spiritualist dog attempting to communicate with Curly's long-dead mother. Finding Dupree as evasive if not as dishonest as Patrick, Curly doubts whether he can solve the question of his sister's disappearance and already considers abandoning his investigation. Dupree, meanwhile, proves how accurate Jenny's statements about the dangers to women are when he assaults her at the club.

When Jenny meets Curly at the railway station he looks more and more like a City man; he carries a briefcase and an umbrella. Indeed, he has been to London to see about a job with an insurance firm and to claim his trunks from storage. Curly obviously is thinking of getting out of the arms business and possibly settling down to respectability in Guildford. For the second time, Jenny senses Curly's lack of resolve.

Jenny now explains to Curly the conspiracy to dispossess Malloy's mother. Mrs. Malloy signed her home over to her son to avoid inheritance taxes. While developers bought the rest of the block in central Guildford, Malloy had his mother certified as insane so that he could take possession of the property. While in the psychiatric institute, Mrs.

Malloy once asked Sarah to run an errand to the house, but Sarah only found "seventeen floors of prestige offices crowned with an antique supermarket" (68). Sarah thereby stumbled upon the conspiracy between Malloy and Patrick, both of whom could profit hugely from the sale of Malloy's mother's home to property speculators. Malloy had his mother institutionalized to obtain control of the property; Patrick provided the investment capital. In hopes of exposing the swindle to the press, Sarah turned to Dupree. But Dupree saw that he, too, could cash in by blackmailing not only Malloy, but Patrick as well. At this point Curly ironically says, "I'm moving down here. Get a job. Get a house. I like the atmosphere" (70). But when Curly announces that he does not plan to confront his father, Jenny simply walks away from him. As earlier, on the Crumbles, Curly's refusal to pursue the investigation and expose Patrick negates any chance of a relationship with Jenny.

When Curly again meets Dupree on the hospital grounds, Dupree pulls his knife on him; Curly then pulls a gun. Curly humiliates and bullies Dupree to admit that Patrick intimidated Malloy in order to obtain Mrs. Malloy's property. When Malloy was home alone, the fuses stolen, a fierce German shepherd was set loose in the house. Malloy, waging "the fight of his life" (75), killed the dog. Dupree then blackmailed Patrick by threatening to tell Sarah that Patrick intimidated Malloy and financed the building development. Even though Patrick met Dupree's demands, Sarah knew that Patrick and Malloy conspired and turned to Dupree to expose them. But when Dupree failed to do so, the ubiquity of corruption (and possibly simple fear) drove Sarah to the brink of madness.

In Curly's final confrontation with his father, Patrick explains that Malloy dumped the dog's corpse on his doorstep as if to assert himself. Nonetheless, the deal was made: Malloy's mother was institutionalized by her own son; Patrick secured the development's financing; the high rise replaced Mrs. Malloy's home. Curly also discovers that Patrick is responsible for Sarah's disappearance, not because he killed her, but because he abandoned her—left her on the Crumbles—so he would not miss a meeting in the City.

Patrick acted with such premeditated care that he can be linked neither to Malloy's dispossession of his own mother nor to Sarah's disappearance. By sacrificing a mother and a daughter to their own greed, Malloy and Patrick confirm Curly's suspicion that "it's as if we *need* so many dead—like axle grease—to make civilization work at all" (37). Curly abandons his code and enters into complicity when he finally decides to spare his father. "All I would be doing," he says, "would be to bang down my tiny flag on the same mountain-side as Sarah" (84). By refusing for the third time to expose Patrick, Curly loses Jenny.

Here, as throughout the play, characters sublimate their sense of responsibility, primarily by making others complicit. Curly recounts an episode when as children he and Sarah dropped a poodle off a tower—a deed that Curly describes as the "only barbaric thing I've ever done": "We released [the dog] at either end, at exactly the same moment—it's the firing squad idea—you don't know who's responsible" (35). That episode becomes emblematic of the shared and supposedly diffused responsibility that mitigates guilt.

Characters   Curly recalls the hard-boiled detectives of Ross Macdonald and Dashiell Hammett who live by a code, uniquely their own and rigorously held, in place of conventional morality. The implication, borne out by Curly and all the men in *Knuckle*, is that conventional values are a hoax. Rejecting the respectability that Patrick epitomizes, Curly's code focuses on a clearly and frequently enunciated principle: there is no "pleasure that isn't more pleasurable for being denied" (46). Curly abstains from many pleasures—alcohol, cigarettes, and sex—because they might weaken him. Once he falls in love with Jenny, however, he intends to indulge in at least one of those pleasures.

Until the end of the play, Curly defines himself by being everything that Patrick is not. But ultimately the security of working for an insurance company appeals to Curly, as does Jenny. Like Patrick, Curly would like to live in the comfort of Guildford, and in particular to settle in with Jenny, as Patrick has with Grace Dunning. But Curly's acceptance of Patrick's duplicity finally dooms any chance he may have had with Jenny. In the next-to-last scene, Curly and Patrick reinforce each other's understanding of the way of the world:

PATRICK:	The pursuit of money is a force for progress . . .
CURLY:	It's always been the same . . .
PATRICK:	The making of money . . .
CURLY:	The breaking of men.
PATRICK:	The two together. Always. The sound of progress.
CURLY:	The making of money. The breaking of men.

(82)

With that litany, Curly's code is undone. His values are now as conventional as they are hypocritical. By the end of the play Curly truly does become his father's son.

A self-contained, self-made man, Patrick represents the City, respectability, and civilized values. Grace describes him as "a very Christian man" (28). Jenny says that Sarah "was obsessed with her father because he was so complete. Sarah used to say he had a personality like a pebble. There was no way in" (50). In fact, Sarah became involved with Malloy precisely because he resembled her father. Patrick is also noteworthy for his cultural refinement: his favorite author is Henry James; as he peruses a musical score, he imagines the power of a performance.

Unlike the men who are associated with hypocrisy, all of the women in this play are associated with outmoded values. Grace Dunning, Patrick's housekeeper and consort, asks Curly: "I wonder why all the words my generation believed in—words like honour and loyalty—are now just a joke" (36). Jenny thinks that men assault women because they are the last repository of goodness: "I expect to be bumped, bruised, followed, assaulted, stared at and propositioned for the rest of my life, while at the same time offering sanctuary, purity, reassurance, prestige—the only point of loveliness in men's ever-darkening lives" (66).

Like her brother, Sarah never appreciated the importance of tact and duplicity. Jenny reports that "Sarah thought everyone should know everything" (31)—a phrase that echoes throughout the play and a belief that Curly would like to, but cannot, claim as his own (79). Curly's choice at the end is clearly between Patrick and Jenny. In defiance of his own code and the audience's expectations, he chooses the former.

Images   *Knuckle* is full of images of violence: Jenny held at knife point by Dupree; the poodle dropped off a tower; a vicious dog let loose in Malloy's house; Malloy's suicide—to say nothing of Curly's career as a gunrunner. Many of the images of violence are directly linked, as in *Lay By,* with sex: the 1924 murder on the Crumbles; Malloy's visits to the whipping parlors; Dupree's attack on Jenny; Sarah's and Jenny's reports of being anonymously brutalized and sexually assaulted. Jenny, in fact, argues that the success of her relationship with Malloy, by which she came to inherit the Shadow of the Moon Club, depended on their not having sex.

The friendship between Jenny and Sarah grows out of their shared perception of the world as a "plush abattoir" (23). On the Crumbles

with Curly, who describes the scene as the "loveliest it gets" (57), Jenny
offers this perception: "I see heavy scowls and fists raised in anger, and I
see tears of sorrow and indignation. I see men with axes in their backs,
acid streaming off their skins, needles in their eyes, tripping on barbed
wire, falling on broken bottles. . . . I see the living dead" (54). As
Jenny suggests, women are often brutalized precisely because of their
innocence. When Dupree grabs Jenny he says to her: "This is a knife.
Kiss me" (65); and later, "I find your innocence unforgivable. Take off
your clothes" (66). A letter presumed to be from Sarah warns: "At all
costs fight innocence. Forbid ignorance. Startle your children. Appal
your mothers. Know everything. . . . I have twice been debauched in
the open road" (86). Patrick sought to prevent Sarah's knowing everything and to preserve his image in her eyes. He confesses to Curly, "My
daughter should not be given the chance to doubt—we were honest
men. . . . I had to buy Dupree. Do you understand? For her sake" (79–
80). But Sarah has long since seen through his hypocrisy.

The violent action and language of *Knuckle* is matched with images of
corruption, swindle, blackmail, and extortion. In the very first episode
of the play Curly orders Jenny a drink and, when he asks to see the
dispenser, discovers that he is deliberately being given short measures.
Of England, Curly says, "I found this country was a jampot for swin-
dlers and cons and racketeers" (55). Later he explains the ubiquity of
swindle to Jenny: "Newspapers can be bought, judges can be leant on,
politicians can be stuffed with truffles and cognac. Life's a racket" (71).
And, Curly tells Jenny, malevolence is as deliberate as it is widespread:

The horror of the world is there are no excuses left. There was a time when
men who ruined other men, could claim they were ignorant or simple or
believed in God, or life was very hard, or we didn't know what we were doing,
but now everybody knows the tricks, the same shabby hands have been played
over and over, and men who persist in old ways of running their countries or
their lives, those men now do it in the full knowledge of what they're doing.
So that at last greed and selfishness and cruelty stand exposed in white neon:
men are bad because they want to be. No excuses left. (71)

These images of corruption in society bear directly on Curly's capitulation and Sarah's disappearance. Jenny says that it would not have taken
much to precipitate Sarah's suicide: "It would only have needed the
barest suggestion. Sarah, just put your head under the water. Moving
from grey to grey. . . . She would have covered herself with kerosene

and set light to it. To win your affection" (51). Madness is a profound threat to someone as vulnerable as Sarah. During his second encounter with Patrick, Curly tells him: "But given that she's dead you want her murdered because then it's nobody's fault except some poor psychopath and there's nothing anyone can do about those. Whereas if she killed herself she's going to squat on your shoulders for the rest of your life" (42). For Patrick, responsibility shared is not his responsibility.

By the end of the play we presume from her letter that Sarah is alive, but attention has shifted from the question of Sarah's death to that of her (and Jenny's) disaffection. Metaphorically, her disaffection is her death—because she has lost sight of the possibility of innocence and goodness.

Knuckle is closer to homage than parody. Its improbable and convoluted plot as well as Curly's code and language all evoke the expectations of the detective/thriller genre. But Hare consistently, almost methodically, refutes those expectations: Curly capitulates; Sarah was not murdered; not even momentarily is justice done. *Knuckle* is the single work among Hare's early plays that clearly anticipates the direction of his playwriting. In examining the impossibility of living "within this system without doing yourself moral damage," *Knuckle,* Hare says, "concludes that there *is* such a thing as moral value."[6] What Patrick finds most offensive is behavior he considers vulgar, loud, or indecorous—precisely the behavior of both Curly and Sarah. Mistaking bad taste for immorality, Patrick sees nothing immoral in either his property swindles or his hypocrisy. The institutionalization of Malloy's mother, Malloy's suicide, and Sarah's disappearance fail to disturb Patrick's conscience. Although he is responsible for or complicit in all three, his self-deception is so profound as to admit no possibility of guilt. As in *The Great Exhibition* and *Teeth 'n' Smiles,* a human brokerage prevails in *Knuckle.*

After a production at the Oxford Playhouse in January 1974, *Knuckle* transferred to the Comedy Theatre in London and became the first of Hare's plays to reach the West End. The production, directed by Michael Blakemore, starred Edward Fox as Curly and Kate Nelligan as Jenny. The London reviews were mixed. Jonathan Hammond judged that Hare "succeeds almost completely"[7] in reworking the L.A. detective genre and transplanting it to Surrey. Apparently expecting another politically relevant play, Michael Billington wrote that "the inherent melodrama of the pulp thriller seriously undermines the attack on the genuine uses of property speculation."[8] That the happy Hollywood

ending was within such easy reach of, but denied, audiences probably
did little to help the play's commercial value.

Teeth 'n' Smiles

Written some six years after its subject and setting, the salad days of
1969, *Teeth 'n' Smiles* examines the subculture of youth and rock 'n'
roll—one supposedly free of the conventional restraints of society—
only to discover the ubiquity of the class structure and the death of
ideals. Its characters share the futility and despair of Lesley, the teenager in *Lay By*, in a context that offers few alternatives.

Although the rock band booked at the Jesus College Ball at Cambridge University on 9 June 1969 is already more than an hour late in
arriving for the concert, no one makes any effort to get on the stage.
Maggie, the lead singer, arrives unconscious from drink, slung over the
shoulder of Snead the porter, and is unceremoniously hauled off to be
revived. The band members prepare their drugs, entertain lurid offers
from groupies, and pass the time exchanging bits of worthless trivia.

Arthur, a song writer who parted company with the band several
years earlier, has come to see Maggie, his former protégé and lover.
From Laura, the band's assistant, Arthur learns how miserably Maggie
and the band are doing. Their fees do not even cover their expenses, but
Maggie—who "likes to keep busy"[9]—hopes to reach San Francisco "on
her knees" (16) in the near future.

All of the delays are supposedly caused by the need for a single plug.
Because they are artists ("You don't ask Oistrakh to go out and strangle
the cat" [15]), the band members refuse to fix it and refuse to allow a
medical student and the concert organizer, Anson, to fix it either. The
exasperating delays and pointless trivia, as well as the first scene, end as
the band finally takes the stage performing "Close to Me."

After a disastrous first set, Anson prepares to interview Maggie, who
has memorized the details of her biography for just such occasions:
"Mother born in Hitchin, father born in Hatfield, so they met half way
and lived all their life in Stevenage. That's how my interview begins"
(34). Drifting in and out of the text of her prepared interview, she
occasionally reveals something of the truth, most important that she
met Arthur when she was seventeen and that he "invent[ed] me" (38)
the way Svengali invented Trilby. Maggie is full of self-pity and desolation: "I only sleep with very stupid men . . . they never understand a
word I say. That makes me trust them. So each one gets told a different

secret, some terrible piece of my life that only they will know. Some
separate . . . awfulness" (40).

Once the interview lurches to a halt, the band takes up another
pastime: "The game is: I read from the London telephone directory. You
lot remain completely silent. The first person to make a sound is
disqualified. The winner is the person who can stand it the longest"
(42). This exercise in futility is interrupted by the arrival of the band's
manager, Saraffian, with his latest discovery, Randolph. Saraffian believes that Maggie drinks "to stop any nasty little outbreaks of happiness among her acquaintances" (45). When Laura presses Saraffian
about Arthur's presence, Saraffian says Arthur came of his own volition:
"The boy adored her. Now he feels responsible" (46). Laura, who (like
Arthur) genuinely cares for Maggie, tells Saraffian that he lets "people
die to avoid cliché" (46)—that, in fact, is his metier as an agent and
promoter who loves the vulgarity and destructiveness of rock 'n' roll.

As in Beckett's *Waiting for Godot,* a sense of suspended animation
hangs over the play. Enervation and boredom lead the characters to
alcohol, drugs, music, casual sex—anything that might momentarily
break the tedium. Something better may come along, but it seems
unlikely. Maggie speaks of waiting for a revolution to occur:

> *MAGGIE:*   I mean, if there was going to be a revolution it would have
>   happened by now. I don't think 1970'll be the big year. I
>   mean the real revolution will have to be . . .
>
> *LAURA:*   Inside?
>
> *MAGGIE:*   Gimme the bottle.
>
>   (50)

Somehow the band musters its energies to appear for a second set.
Maggie begins by carrying on a nonsensical conversation with the
audience that matches self-pity with contempt. After the set, as Maggie is again hauled off, this time by Nash, Saraffian wastes little time in
breaking his news to her: "Arthur would like to be free of you. He
would like to set up a home with Laura. Yes. And you're sacked" (56).
Immediately after that, Snead the porter announces: "This is a raid.
You're all busted" (56).

While the police interview band members offstage, Anson shows
Arthur an item of curiosity intended to provoke some reaction in the
deadened sensibilities of the band: a finger severed from a corpse. But
even this gruesome trophy provokes little response. Saraffian asks the

band members where they have hidden their drugs; the answer is, in Maggie's carpetbag. Despite their taste for the outré, nothing—not the police raid, not a severed finger, not Maggie's imminent arrest—disturbs the band's torpor. Having cultivated the outrageous, none of them can respond, let alone feel outrage.

The band will not be paid unless they perform their third set. With Maggie unwilling to perform, Saraffian substitutes Randolph. But there is no one left to hear them play. Arthur confronts Saraffian with the question of what will happen to Maggie, but that is interrupted by Maggie's burning down a tent. Arthur and Maggie finally have their moment together, but it quickly becomes plain that there is no hope of renewing the relationship between them. In the play's final scene, amid the smoldering rubble, Saraffian and the band's keyboardist congratulate Maggie on setting the fire. Destructive and pointless, her gesture nonetheless is original. Taken off to prison on drug charges, Maggie leaves telling them: "Remember. I'm nobody's excuse. If you love me, keep on the move" (85). Through where-are-they-now projections, Hare reveals that Peyote, the bass guitarist, died à la Jim Morrison four years later; the others remain alive, well, and living in England. The play ends with "Maggie's Song" asking for "Last orders on the *Titanic*" (91–92).

Characters   For outsiders like Anson, the eager medical student who interviews Maggie, the rock world appears exciting and authentic. For those inside it, the rock demimonde offers escape through adulation, drugs, and alcohol. Many of them, like Inch, who injects Preludin (an amphetamine), have simply drifted into an unreflective self-destruction. But for the principal characters—Maggie, Arthur, Laura, and Saraffian—there is a consciousness of their decline that reveals despair. Much like *The Great Exhibition, Plenty, Dreams of Leaving,* and *Wetherby, Teeth 'n' Smiles* shows generation after generation of the British disheartened, disillusioned, and disaffected. In towns and cities, for the bourgeosis and the upper classes, the only alternatives seem to be exploitation of others or self-destruction.

Saraffian is cut from the same fabric as Alfred Bagley and Lambert La Roux. As Maggie tells him, he does not care what product he markets: soapflakes or rock stars are both merchandise to him. Although he harbors romantic memories of the heyday of rock ("It'll never get better than 1956" [52]), Saraffian has no scruples about exploiting anyone. His Hobbesian approach emanates, not surprisingly, from an experi-

ence during the war. Saraffian found himself among the rich and fashionable in "a perfect reproduction of the ballroom" (82) of the *Titanic* in
the Café de Paris on 9 March 1941, the night German bombs destroyed
the club. As Saraffian lies wounded in the ruins he sees a man moving
about the rubble and corpses: "I close my eyes. One comes near. I can
smell his breath. He touches my hand. He then removes the ring from
my finger. He goes. He is looting the dead. And my first thought is:
I'm with you, pal. I cannot help it, that was my first thought. Even
here, even now, even in fire, even in blood, I am with you in your scarf
and cap, slipping the jewels from the hands of the corpses. I'm with
you" (83). Moreover, Saraffian, like Archie Maclean in *Licking Hitler,* is
always fighting a class war. As he tells Maggie: "There is a war going
on. All the time. A war of attrition" (84). Maggie sees this as nothing
more than Saraffian's "nice little class war" (84)—an excuse for his
misanthropy and exploitation of others. But for Saraffian life is this
war, the survival of the fittest. In *Teeth 'n' Smiles* some characters barely
survive; others seek out their own destruction. Implicit is yet another
front in the class war: the Cambridge students for whom the band
performs are likely to assume a privileged position in British society,
while their less privileged contemporaries, the band members, have
only wretched prospects.

A former student as well as a musician, Arthur straddles both worlds
in his attempt to escape. Combining what Maggie calls intelligence
and Saraffian identifies as a sense of responsibility, Arthur left Maggie
and the rock world. He, in fact, wrote several of the songs Maggie
continues to perform. With nostalgia, Arthur recalls first meeting
Maggie when he was reading music at Jesus College, Cambridge (where
Hare received his degrees), and Maggie was a sixteen-year-old folk-
singer. He left Maggie, but comes back to her saying, "I can't live
without you. I can't get through the day" (80). Maggie simply tells
him that she loved him as he used to be. To which he responds, "But
it's you that's made me the way I am now." And she answers: "I know.
That's what's called irony" (80).

Although innocent of the drug charge, Maggie accepts the role of
scapegoat as the apotheosis of her victimization. In fulfillment of her
self-destructive inclinations, she says that she will not mind going to
prison. Hare even attributes to Maggie a clear choice: "[Maggie]
chooses to go to prison because it will give her an experience of suffering which is bound in her eyes to be more worthwhile than the life she
could lead outside."[10]

Maggie makes much of her suffering; it's even part of her press release: "The quality of the singing depends on the quality of the pain" (39). Like Susan Traherne in *Plenty,* she combines impulses toward self-destruction and self-pity with real suffering. Theirs is a conscious descent into despair. And as Susan does in the final lines of *Plenty,* Maggie vividly (though drunkenly) recalls the promise she once believed and the disillusionment she now knows:

I was six, I think, I had a village there by the riverbank, doll village with village shop, selling jelly beans, little huts, little roads. I took the local priest down there, I wanted him to consecrate the little doll church. The sun was shining and he took my head in his hands. He said, inside this skull the most beautiful piece of machinery that God ever made. He said, a fair-haired English child, you will think and feel the finest things in the world. The sun blazed and his hands enclosed my whole skull. (72)

Like Susan, Maggie once believed in a future of almost unlimited happiness and fulfillment. As if in refutation of that idea, both Susan and Maggie cultivate their own misery and suffering and cannot face the world without drugs or alcohol.

Themes and Images   Hare engenders a strong sense of waste, futility, and enervation in *Teeth 'n' Smiles.* Twice he alludes to the *Titanic.*[11] The object of both the games the band members play—first, exchanging worthless trivia, and later reading from the London phone directory—is simply to pass the time with entirely inconsequential scraps of information that underscore the pointlessness and vacuity of their lives.

Maggie clearly drinks to escape, but she is not the only one aware of the self-destruction encoded in this world. Arthur recalls another rock musician who played at a deafening level: "I said to him, why the hell don't you wear muffs? In eighteen months you're going to be stone deaf. He said: that's why we play so loud. The louder we play, the sooner we won't be able to hear. I can see us all. Rolling down the highway into middle age. Complacency. Prurience. Sadism. Despair" (88). Given the youth of the characters, the sense of waste is even keener. Only Saraffian has direction in his life, and he finds it in the exploitation of others. The musicians speak of the "pain"—the prerequisite for successful music—and devote much of their energies to making themselves miserable, as if to cultivate their pain.

The setting and time of the play ironically counterpoint the inability of these characters to channel their energies in any constructive way. What they do, they do badly. Though they are part of the generation associated with political and personal rebellion, the revolution that Maggie and Laura once anticipated is not about to take place. For these characters, the future holds only empty promises and excuses for their own self-destructive impulses.

Initial Critical Reception   *Teeth 'n' Smiles,* the only one of Hare's plays initially performed at the Royal Court, opened on 2 September 1975 in a production directed by Hare, starring Jack Shepherd as Arthur, Helen Mirren as Maggie, and Dave King as Saraffian. Perhaps the venue alone put several critics in mind of a comparison with John Osborne's *The Entertainer,* another Royal Court play that uses a spent, cynical performer to epitomize England. Charles Lewsen in the London *Times* offered a typically mixed review which praised the play's humor and the performance of Saraffian by Dave King but faulted Hare for not further developing the image of England as the *Titanic.* [12] In *Plays and Players* Ronald Bryden criticized Hare for "an intrusion of himself on his creation by trying too hard to be magisterial," but admired his insight "that the pop millennium never arrived, never had the political stamina to do so, but turned instead to a generation of self-exposers flogging lost, frenzied hopes for a few years of cash and glitter." [13]

Summation

The characters of these plays are both more complex and more reticent than those in Hare's earlier plays and collaborations. Both plays portray worlds normally presumed to be pleasant, attractive, and festive as menacing, corrupt, and dangerous. In them characters speak a stylized, often elliptical language indicative of how removed they are from ordinary life.

In his 1978 lecture at Cambridge Hare described his own writing in this way:

I write love stories. Most of my plays are that. Over and over I have written about romantic love, because it never goes away. And the view of the world it provides, the dislocation it offers, is the most intense experience that many people know on earth.

And I write comedy because . . . such ideas as the one I have just uttered make me laugh.

And I write about politics because the challenge of communism, in however debased and ugly a form, is to ask whether the criteria by which we have [been] brought up are right."[14]

Knuckle and *Teeth 'n' Smiles* mark an important departure for Hare from the broad satirical works of his apprenticeship in the theater. Here his distinctive themes and character types emerge with greater clarity and subtlety. His treatment of madness, especially as it threatens his women characters, will be more fully explored in his next play, *Plenty*.

Chapter Five
Plenty

Plenty deserves to be Hare's best-known work, not only because it is among his finest plays but because it epitomizes his themes and character types. Like many of his works of the 1970s, *Plenty* deals with specifically British experiences and personalities. In the *New Yorker* in early 1983, Hare defended his tendency to generalize about the British character: "You see, I feel that the British walk in a certain way. They hold their heads down in a certain way. They seem to be saying, 'There is no use in doing anything, no point in trying.' "[1] In the American edition of *Plenty* Hare cautioned: "To those of you who perform the play abroad, I can only say that its Englishness is of the essence. To me, when an actor asks why he does something, it is a perfectly good answer to say 'Because you are English.' Irony is central to English humour, and as a people we are cruel to each other, but always quietly."[2] Susan Traherne, the protagonist of *Plenty,* defines herself in distinctly British terms and is defined by her experience of British history. She is ultimately destroyed by her own idealism; the hopes and dreams of her youth eventually yield to the despair and madness of middle age. Her experiences as a British intelligence courier in France during World War II whet an appetite for adventure that proves inherently insatiable.

Plenty begins at Easter in 1962 as Susan walks out on her husband Brock and turns their house over to her friend Alice. Hare provides virtually no exposition regarding this opening situation; instead, he offers the episodic scenes that follow Susan between 1943 and 1962. There is little transition between these scenes—the unity of the play lies in Susan's character and, to a much lesser extent, in her friendship with Alice and the succession of historical settings.

In St. Benoît in France nineteen years earlier Susan, a courier for Special Operations Executive (S.O.E.) although only eighteen years old, meets Lazar, a British operative who has parachuted into Occupied France. From her youngest appearance, Susan combines strength and vulnerability. One of very few British women working undercover in Occupied France, she collapses in Lazar's arms, telling him about her lover, Tony, who has been captured by the Germans and sent to Buchenwald. Her anxiety and tears make her seem more like an eighteen-year-old girl than an experienced agent. Horrified by the prospect of Tony's death, she is a jumble of contradictions and fears for her own life. First she advises Lazar just to obey the rules, but then wonders "What's the point of following the rules if. . . ."[3] There are clearly two sides to Susan; they exist simultaneously and are never reconciled.

Susan next appears in the British embassy in Brussels in 1947 to make arrangements because of the death of her supposed husband. Sir Leonard Darwin, the British ambassador, and Raymond Brock, the third secretary, discuss with Susan the arrangements for Tony Radley's funeral and burial. Of course, Tony is not her husband, but the agent she mentioned to Lazar in the previous scene. Despite the attachment she earlier showed to Tony, Susan tells Brock that she was "barely his mistress" (146); they were simply on "a holiday abroad." Now in control of her emotions, Susan prides herself on her unsentimental, uncompromised attitude.

Susan persuades Brock to contact Tony's widow because "it seemed a shocking injustice when he fell in the lobby, unjust for him of course, but also unjust for me, alone, a long way from home, and worst of all for his wife, bitterly unfair if she had to have the news from me. Unfair for life. And so I approached the embassy" (147). Brock and Susan begin an affair based, ironically enough, on the lie that Brock agrees to tell Tony's widow.

Three months later Brock visits Susan and her eccentric roommate, Alice, in London. The drab austerity of Britain after the war contrasts with the elaborate pink package that Brock brings Susan. Brock believes his talent for tripling his financial investments epitomizes an enormous prosperity that awaits them all. Susan, meanwhile, knows a vastly different reality in 1947: food rationing, queues, powdered eggs. What Hare shows of their courtship only suggests how unsuited Susan and Brock are for each other. Brock is ill at ease with Susan's bohemian friend Alice; Susan openly mocks his diplomatic assignments as trivial and ludicrous. But his comparative wealth and glamour provide an alternative to her drab, impecunious life. As she waxes nostalgic about Lazar and the war, Susan tells Brock that she thinks they should spend the winter apart. When Brock suggests that she come to Brussels with him, she says that she could not possibly leave the job she earlier described to Alice as frustrating and unrewarding.

In 1951 Susan, still living in London, meets Mick, a merchandizer, to watch the fireworks celebrating the Festival of London. Mick is an East Ender from a distinctly "different class" (164). The subject of their bargaining soon changes from cheese graters to a child, as Susan proposes that he father her child, but on terms she sets forth as methodically as those of any business deal. She wants nothing to do with compromise and asks, "why should I have to make some sad and decorous marriage just to have a child" (162). She promises him no demands beyond impregnation—neither emotional nor material. For eighteen months Susan and Mick try, unsuccessfully, to conceive a child. When Susan rejects his attempt to have anything other than a sexual relationship with her, Mick is the first of many characters to see her as mad: "You [Susan and Alice] are cruel and dangerous. . . . She [Susan] is actually mad" (170). Susan silences Mick by firing her revolver at him.

Sometime between the beginning of 1953 and the autumn of 1956, Susan and Brock marry. Later Susan explains that after shooting at Mick, she was sent to a sanitarium, where Brock visited her and proposed. Again, Brock's greatest attraction is that he provides an alternative to Susan's miserable circumstances.

Susan could hardly find an environment less suited to her restlessness and disdain for convention than the diplomatic world. At a dinner party in their fashionable Knightsbridge home in October 1956, Susan lashes out against Darwin, now a senior diplomat at work on the Suez crisis. She begs for a confrontation, but Darwin, although obviously antagonized by his hostess, refuses to argue with her. Much more than simply impolite, Susan stages her attack before the bewildered dinner guests in what Alice labels her "psychiatric cabaret" (177). Darwin asks Brock if mental illness is Susan's problem: "In the diplomatic service it isn't as if a mad wife is any kind of professional disadvantage. On the contrary, it almost guarantees promotion" (174). Less and less in control of her life and more inclined to outrageous gestures, Susan is obviously deteriorating. After Darwin's departure, she orders yet another dinner prepared and rants at no one in particular: "There is plenty. Shall we eat again?" (179).

As a matter of principle and honor, Darwin resigns his post over the British handling of the Suez crisis. Despite his past loyalty and service, he is shunned by his former associates. Brock, Susan, and Alice are virtually the only ones to attend his funeral in 1961. Once back in Britain from Brock's posting in Iran, Susan refuses to leave London—an act that quickly becomes tantamount to Brock's desertion of his diplomatic post.

Susan again speaks her mind when she confronts the personnel director of the Foreign Service, Sir Andrew Charleson, six months later in January 1962. Once more Susan summons up her bravado for this desperate gambit, but in Charleson she finds the paragon of diplomatic language and evasiveness. When Susan bluntly inquires about her husband's prospects, Charleson replies that "Brock is making haste slowly" (192). In an unctuous burlesque of Hamlet's "Readiness is all" or Edgar's "Ripeness is all," Charleson concludes that "Behaviour is all" (193). In response, Susan announces that she will commit suicide if her husband is not promoted within six days. She accuses Charleson of ruining Brock's career, but closer to the truth is that this, one of her final overreaching bluffs, finally destroys whatever slim chance for advancement Brock might have had.

Soon after Susan's confrontation with Charleson, Brock leaves the diplomatic service and takes an insurance job that he, as well as Susan, despises. In scene 10, set at Easter in 1962 (chronologically just before the first scene of the play), Susan, as restless as she was seventeen years earlier, decides to clean up her life by parting with the material clutter. In her frustration and madness, she destroys valued and valuable possessions and finally decides to strip the paper from the wall. Until this time Brock evenly tolerates Susan's outrages, but finally he bursts out: "Your life is selfish, self-interested gain. That's the most charitable interpretation to hand. You claim to be protecting some personal ideal, always at a cost of almost infinite pain to everyone around you. You are selfish, brutish, unkind" (199). Brock's accusations are hardly groundless, but he has contained or surpressed them for so long that when they flood out, his precision and candor are shocking. Indeed, Susan has always been as she is now. Brock threatens to commit her to a mental hospital, but Susan still has the presence of mind to realize that because of the holiday, he will not be able to contact a doctor. She seizes the moment to sedate him, turn the house over to Alice, and take flight.

In the penultimate scene, set in Blackpool a few months after she leaves Brock, Susan and Lazar meet in a shabby seaside hotel. They still associate each other with the romance and danger they knew in France during the war. Both have faced disappointment and disillusionment, although Susan implores him not to speak of his experience. Unsatisfied by his life, Lazar says: "What I'd hoped for, at the time I returned [was] some sort of edge to the life that I lead. Some feeling their death was

worthwhile" (204). Like Susan, he never found any direction and sees
his life as a series of compromises. But she only wants to recapture a
moment with the man who dropped from the sky in France nearly
twenty years ago. Unable to face the man Lazar has become, she smokes
marijuana until she passes out.

The final scene returns to St. Benoît, two months after D-Day.
Susan, again a teenager, radiates hope, not only for herself, but for
England and all the world: "Have you seen anything as beautiful as
this? . . . things will quickly change. We [the English] have grown
up. We will improve our world" (205–6). More than any other lines in
the play, these express Susan's optimism and hope. Overcoming death
and winning the war, fills her and, by implication, all the English,
with a hope that is doomed to disappointment.

Characters   Susan wants life on her own terms and none other.
Her rebellion against conventional behavior provides Susan with a
unique identity, an easy distinction between herself and the dreariness
she sees not only in postwar England but also in Brock's desolate
diplomatic postings. But her self-reliance, sense of adventure, and
belief that she is above and beyond the trappings of convention only
thinly veil her vulnerability.

Mick, the twenty-year-old from the East End whom she selects to
sire her child, is victimized by Susan's frightening ability to separate
love and sex absolutely. Initially Susan tells Mick that she cannot
approach men she knows with such a request because "they are very
limited in their ideas, they are frightened of the unknown, they want a
quiet life where sex is either sport or duty but absolutely nothing in
between" (162–63). Yet Susan sees sex in essentially these same terms.
She hopes for an adventure—preferably a clandestine and dangerous
one—to quicken her sensibilities and heighten her experience. Her
romantic affair with Lazar retains an authenticity that she struggles to
replicate. For nineteen years she idealizes her brief encounter with Lazar
so that nothing in reality, surely not even Lazar himself, can match it.

Throughout her life, Susan stands on the brink of madness. Her first
breakdown comes sometime after the end of her relationship with
Mick; subsequent nervous collapses punctuate her life as well as Brock's
Foreign Service record. One breakdown provides her with an excuse for
staying in London after Darwin's funeral.

There is a fundamental ambiguity in Hare's presentation of Susan.
On the one hand, she is frustrated, trapped, and unfulfilled; on the

other, she is selfish, insatiable, and unreasonable. She hurts many of the people, especially men—Brock, Mick, Darwin—who care for her. Although Susan finds her work pointless and dull, she uses it as an excuse, both with Brock (in scene 4) and with Mick (in scene 6) to avoid emotional involvement. The ambiguity of Susan also owes much to the contradiction within herself and the disparity between what she says and what she does. She wants "to change everything" (153), but finds only meaningless employment. She hates compromise, but marries Brock. She despises conventionality but lives in diplomatic bastions of politesse. She passionately seeks justice but makes no commitments. She is vulnerable yet destructive. Hare believes that this "ambiguity is central to the idea of the play. The audience is asked to make its own mind up about each of the actions. In the act of judging the audience learns something about its own values."[4]

Alice and Susan share a restlessness and dissatisfaction with life, but the contrast between them is at least as strong as their shared disdain for convention. Alice refuses compromises and accepts the consequences of her actions. Flitting between one grand scheme and another, Alice first announces her intention to become a great author and believes that an artist must experience the degradations of life. Alice ultimately decides to end her solipsism, saying that "it may be time to do good" (197), and devotes her energies to a series of social work projects: teaching, aiding unwed mothers, helping battered wives. Susan always admires Alice's freedom and independence, but by this point Susan's self-absorption and drug dependency detach her from the purpose Alice seems to find in life.

The men in the play—Brock, Darwin, and Mick—are neither as complex nor as unconventional as Susan and Alice. All of them seek a security that Alice and Susan find suffocating. Each is in some way admirable: Brock seeks to rescue Susan from her madness; Mick falls in love with her; Darwin resigns his diplomatic post to register his protest against the British actions during the Suez crisis. Yet none of them can hope to measure up to Susan's romantic idealization of Lazar.

Although Lazar, known only by his wartime code name, appears only briefly, the similarity of his experiences and Susan's suggests the pervasive disillusionment of the British in the postwar era. That his life so closely parallels Susan's indicates that her madness, self-destruction, and rage are not simply "psychiatric cabaret," but to some extent typical of the British. Seen in the context of Hare's other plays, Susan's disillusionment becomes emblematic of her as well as Hare's generation.

Historical Context   *Plenty* charts the deterioration of Susan Traherne against landmark events in Britain since World War II. The Festival of Britain (commemorating the centennial of the Great Exposition of 1851) and the Suez crisis become touchstones for the decline of Britain's empire. Charleson alludes to this when confronting Susan in 1962: "The irony is this: we had an empire to administer, there were six hundred of us in this place. Now it's to be dismantled and there are six thousand. As our power declines, the fight among us for access to that power becomes a little more urgent, a little uglier perhaps. As our influence wanes, as our empire collapses, there is little to believe in" (193). During the dinner party in scene 7—set in 1956—Susan taunts Darwin by contrasting her role as a British operative in France during the war with his supposed involvement in the Suez fiasco: "By and large we did make it our business to land in countries where we were wanted" (178). But when Susan first meets Lazar, they argue with a Frenchman over supplies dropped from a plane. Even then he tells them, "Nobody ask you. Nobody ask you to come. *Vous n'êtes pas les bienvenus ici*" (139).

That is not the only challenge to the glories of the S.O.E. operations. When a radio interviewer reports that "it's frequently been alleged that Special Operations was amateurish, its recruitment methods were haphazard, some of its behaviour was rather cavalier" (188), Susan answers that "it was one part of the war from which the British emerge with the greatest possible valour and distinction" (188). In her own way, she, like Darwin, is unable to assess the British role in history in anything less than ideal terms.

Hare's references to the Suez crisis in 1956 are equally telling. Here even Darwin sees the British as operating dishonestly: "I think the entire war is a fraud cooked up by the British as an excuse for seizing the canal" (175). The Suez crisis also marks the low point in British diplomatic history and today is seen as a debacle.

The "plenty" of the play's title refers to Brock's uncanny luck in the stock market and, ironically, to the prosperity of the 1950s that he envisions. Britain did not enjoy the postwar economic boom that America did. Clothing was rationed in Britain until after the Festival of Britain in 1951. But Brock's financial knack assures that he and Susan do have money. As Susan hands over a check to pay for a rich girl's abortion, she tells Alice: "We're rotten with cash" (186). Hare's pun is, of course, intentional: they have plenty of money, but the money has corrupted them. Brock offers a similar understanding: "Too much money. I think that's what went wrong. Something about it corrupts one's will to live" (195). The final scene realizes the cutting irony of the title in expressing the full measure of Susan's hope and idealism after the war. Never again can Susan imagine the emotional plenty she once knew when she had purpose and passion in her life.

Sources and Precedents   Susan stands in a long line of Hare's female protagonists: the greatest affinities lie with Sarah and Jenny in *Knuckle,* Maggie in *Teeth 'n' Smiles,* and Anna in *Licking Hitler.* Like Sarah in *Knuckle,* Susan insists that people should speak their minds and wants to know everything. Like Maggie, she cultivates a sense of doom: doom to loveless marriage, doom to conform to society's expectations, doom to disappointment. Like Anna, she is involved in covert intelligence operations during wartime when, as Hare observes, "sex under such circumstances has a special charge."[5]

And like many of Hare's characters—Maggie, Joanne in *Slag,* and Hammett in *The Great Exhibition*—Susan's imagined suffering leads her to solipsism. So conscious of her pain is she that during their first meeting Brock asks her, "You don't think you wear your suffering a little heavily? This smart club of people you belong to who had a very bad war. . . . I mean I know it must have put you on a different level from the rest of us" (147). Susan's self-absorption turns her inward and makes it impossible for her, unlike Alice, to find fulfillment outside herself.

Susan's closest dramatic kin is Ibsen's Hedda Gabler.[6] Angered or frustrated by virtually every experience in life, both Susan and Hedda marry for reasons that have more to do with material security than with love and find disappointment in their husbands's less-than-spectacular careers. Both, too, are not above creating a scene or an outrage. And although they have the trappings of a "liberated" woman, they fundamentally adhere to superficial conventions, value material comfort, and reject commitment. In this regard, Susan and Hedda are foiled by other women—Alice and Thea, respectively—who do overthrow convention, specifically through commitments to causes and individuals.

Susan and Hedda also wield guns—symbols of their destructive powers that are intended to exact respect and submission. The pistols Hedda inherits from her father figure importantly; ultimately, they are the instruments of Hedda and Lovborg's deaths. The revolver that Susan brandishes is the emblem of her bluff style and desire to outrage. It is her ultimate recourse, but one she uses too frequently. Susan and Hedda share destructive impulses that they finally turn against themselves. Having failed to destroy a world they despise, they destroy themselves: Hedda through suicide; Susan through drugs and despair. The crucial difference between Hedda and Susan is that although they are both frustrated and trapped by their society, Susan's disaffection is emblematic of a distinctly British malaise that also afflicts Lazar and, to a lesser extent, Alice.

Critical Reception   *Plenty* was the first of Hare's plays to appear at Britain's National Theatre, where Hare directed it in the Lyttelton Theatre. The original production starred Kate Nelligan, to whom the play is dedicated, as Susan, Julie Covington as Alice, and Stephen Moore as Brock.

Initial critical response, which ranged from unappreciative to befuddled, relied primarily on a torrent of rhetorical questions. Bernard Levin in nothing less than the London *Sunday Times* asked: "But what does the author want us to think, to feel? What is he saying? What does he believe about his characters are their predicament?"[7] Similarly, W. Stephen Gilbert in *Plays and Players* wondered "Why is Hare here in the Lyttelton?"[8] For Gilbert (and several other critics) *Plenty* "lacks a polemical edge [that] it really needs to cut through."[9] Irving Wardle praised the play as "a work of biting intelligence and highly disciplined structure, carrying conviction on every specific issue it touches," but also asked "What precisely is driving her round the bend in the final scenes?"[10]

Hare also directed *Plenty* for the New York Shakespeare Festival in October 1982. Writing in the *New York Times,* Frank Rich identified the Joseph Papp production as "an explosive theatrical vision of a world that was won and lost during and after World War II."[11] When the production transferred to the Plymouth Theatre, making *Plenty* the first of Hare's plays to reach Broadway, Clive Barnes called it "the best play of the Broadway season so far."[12]

Chapter Six
Plays for Television

Of the media in which he has worked, Hare has good reason for being least comfortable with television. Some of his work for television no longer exists simply because it was erased. Hare's first work for television, *Man above Men,* directed by Alan Clarke, aired on 19 March 1973, no longer exists in the BBC archives and remains unpublished. In the mid-1970s both *Brassneck* and *Fanshen* were adapted for television after their initial stage productions. Hare also vigorously objects to the arbitrary and absurd censorship imposed on television, most notably in the case of Roy Minton's play about the borstal system, *Scum.*[1]

It is difficult to classify *Licking Hitler* as a television film while labeling *Wetherby* a feature film for several reasons. First, both were shot on film stock rather than videotape, a medium Hare dislikes intensely. Not only does videotape present editing problems, but the expectation of the BBC, at least in the early 1970s, was that video productions could be shot in the same studios and with the same scheduling as other programming. (Hare waited a year, until one of the prized film slots opened at the BBC Birmingham, to make *Licking Hitler.*) Second, both were produced by and shown on British television.[2] Third, both—like the films of *Plenty, Dreams of Leaving,* and *Saigon: Year of the Cat*—employed a more extensive rehearsal schedule than typical in either film or television productions. Hare's experience as a theater director led him to the conviction that on videotape "the *performance* is the thing that gets put last and is considered least important. . . . the actor can neither get the 'through line' on his part which he can in the theatre, nor can he get the moment-to-moment steady construction of his part which he can from film."[3]

Licking Hitler

Plenty and *Licking Hitler* are included, along with *Knuckle,* in the Faber & Faber collection of Hare's works called *The History Plays.* Hare notes that he "wrote *Plenty* alongside *Licking Hitler.* . . . some days I would spend the morning writing *Plenty* and the afternoon in the

cutting-room with *Licking Hitler.*"[4] Both works in fact grew directly
out of memoirs written by British agents after World War II. In depict-
ing individuals brutalized and sometimes destroyed by lovelessness,
these works mark a further departure from the broader, more satirical
lines of Hare's earlier plays, especially his early collaborations.

Licking Hitler begins as a military convoy disrupts the perfect peace
and tranquility at an English country manor. The estate, Wendlesham,
has been commandeered for use in the propaganda efforts of the S.O.E.
(Special Operations Executive) during the war. Lord Minton, owner of
the estate, is summarily dispatched to "that squalid wee single end in
Eaton Square"[5] in the heart of London.

Archie Maclean, the author of black propaganda broadcasts designed
to subvert the will of the German people, dictates his latest radio script
to a secretary, Eileen Graham. This particular broadcast denounces Rudolph Hess as a traitor and criminal lunatic. The script's language and
content are deliberately offensive and repulsive: "The greybeard eunuchs
and slug-like parvenues congest and clot the bloodstream of the nation"
(94). Into this situation walks Anna Seaton, niece of the second sea lord
at the Admiralty, an upper class girl of little worldly experience who
brings to the unit a fluency in German acquired during summers spent in
Oberwesel. When Archie assigns her to prepare tea, she wastes a week's
ration of tea trying to do what she has never done before.

At a staff meeting, the unit's superior, Fennel, sets out their goals
and restrictions: security regulations demand the staff's isolation at
Wendlesham; he will provide their only contact with the outside world,
and he will not visit often. The unit's broadcasts purport to be coded
communiqués between two German officers stationed thousands of
miles apart, followed by more intimate exchanges between the com-
rades in arms. These private conversations are intended to foment
unrest and dissatisfaction among the Germans who overhear them. As
Archie tells Anna, the language of the Prussian officer to be played by
Otto must be "rough . . . corrosive . . . obscene" (102). The first
broadcast is hardly a success: When Karl, one of the German-speaking
actors, loses his place in the script, the inauthenticity of the conversation becomes apparent.

That night a drunk and violent Archie bursts into Anna's room. After
he passes out, Anna drags him out in the hall and covers him with a
blanket. The next morning when Anna ventures to mention the event,
Archie bullies her as if to deny anything ever happened. Bizarre routines
set in at Wendlesham: Karl blunders through another broadcast; the

upper-class staff members amuse themselves in upper-class ways—playing croquet and sipping drinks; Anna barricades her door against Archie's intrusions. Anna's isolation and loneliness grows steadily: standing alone in the hall, she implores, "[s]omebody talk to me" (106).

As Hitler prepares to invade Russia, the unit contemplates its response. Langley, the director, argues that the loyal German officer should condemn the invasion as one that Hitler himself advises against in *Mein Kampf*. Archie takes the opposite view, saying that "anything that sounds like propaganda is not good propaganda" (107); if the invasion of Russia is indeed a military blunder, the broadcasts should celebrate the move and assume that it in itself will undermine the Reich as well as stigmatize anyone opposing the decision as a Bolshevik.

Over the weeks, the quality of the broadcasts does improve: Karl becomes a credible actor; Langley is thrilled; Herr Jungke, a German actor borrowed from an internment camp, is rewarded with a glass of sambuca, complete with coffee bean. Anna meanwhile tries to find out something about Archie. The night after she decides not to put the chair against her door, Archie charges into her room and announces "The Scot makes love wi' a broken bottle. An' a great deal a' screamin' " (111). He sleeps with Anna, but when she attempts to talk to him, he simply walks out on her. Although Anna has been bruised during his nighttime assaults, Archie consistently refuses any but the most perfunctory conversation with her. While at work during the days, Archie never hints at his relationship with Anna. He never acknowledges her injuries, her individuality, her loneliness. Anna's growing collection of Archie's whiskey bottles marks the frequency of his visits and the passage of time.

Eileen's and Anna's next assignment is to read letters from Germans mailed to the United States, "to comb through these letters . . . to pick out from the gossip any hard fact, any details of their way of life, any indiscretion" (113) that might prove useful in the broadcasts. The black propaganda efforts now focus on the burgomaster of Cologne. To bolster his slander Archie dutifully consults Krafft-Ebing, Havelock Ellis, and Kleinwort's *Dictionary of Sexual Perversion*. The more perverse the aspersions he can cast on someone he has never met, the greater his satisfaction and his belief in the unit's potential success.

Anna eventually confides to Eileen that she is involved with Archie, although they have "never had a conversation" (120). Eileen believes Archie is "barking mad" (119). When Eileen learns that her brother has been killed in Singapore, she is dispatched with the same haste that characterized Lord Minton's removal. Anna chides Archie for not even saying goodbye to Eileen. His response, justifying his attitude toward his work, provides the best explanation for his actions: "Just . . . get on with it. This house is the war. And I'd rather be anywhere, I'd rather be in France, I'd rather be in the desert, I'd rather be in a Wellington over Berlin, anywhere but here with you and your people in this bloody awful English house . . . but I shall spend it here" (121). Archie's war, like Saraffian's, is a class war waged on intimate terms. Outside his late-night intrusions, Archie continues to refuse any human contact with Anna.

Anna finally complains about broadcasts intended "to convince an army which we believe has just sustained the most appalling losses in the history of human warfare that those of them who have managed to escape death are on the point of being consumed with venereal disease" (122). She then asks Langley if he thinks that Archie is insane. But Langley lashes out at her, saying that they must bring to their work "the same vigour, the same passion, the same intelligence" that Joseph Goebbels and the German propagandists bring to theirs. And, he continues, "if it means covering the whole continent in obloquy and filth . . . then that is what we shall do" (123). Accusing Anna of making sexual advances to Archie, Langley says she has "unbalanced one of our most gifted writers" (123). Threatening to speak with Anna's father, Langley demands her resignation.

The final broadcast stages Otto's death and marks the end of this operation. From voice-over narration we hear of the prosperity and success of the operation's staff: Fennel becomes a Labour cabinet member; Langley writes thrillers remarkable for their "sustained passages of sexuality and violence" (125); Eileen opens a chain of employment agencies; and Archie becomes a successful film director. Anna, like Susan Traherne, frustrated by years in advertising, grows "increasingly distressed at the compromises forced on her by her profession" (126). But more like Alice than Susan, Anna "resigned and announced her intention to live an honest life" (126).

Characters   Like many of Hare's characters, those in *Licking Hitler* engage in futile pursuits. The British agents, especially Anna, know how unlikely success is. Their propaganda is not simply mudslinging; it is mudslinging into the void. As Fennel admits to his staff: "I'm afraid you will know very little about the success or failure of your work. You are throwing stones into a pond which is a very long way away. And there will be almost no ripples" (98). Of course there are more than mere ripples, but probably not among the German people. The group's activities do more to subvert the values and morale of the British agents producing the propaganda than those of the German people. Observing the niceties of British decorum is fundamentally at odds with creating scurrilous propaganda. Their very proximity to the filth they manufacture taints the perceptions of these characters, especially Archie.

Archie's childhood was neither comfortable nor secure. "By the time the war came," says Eileen, "he was on one of the national dailies. Fought his way up . . . [from] Poverty. Terrible. He comes from Glasgow, from the Red Clyde" (111). This is the very background that Archie much later sentimentalizes in one of his documentary films. As Fennel observes of Archie with detachment: "The Celtic race, you know: a cloven-hoofed people. They do seem to be fighting quite a different war" (115). Archie's war is partly a class war, partly a war on innocence. Under pressure to make his scripts as vicious as possible, his own viciousness finds an easy target, one that combines class privilege and innocence, in Anna Seaton.

Anna in many ways epitomizes what Archie most despises in the English. Sheltered by a provincial upbringing and her family's wealth, Anna joins the service out of a sense of duty and a desire to preserve the only values she knows—those of a privileged English life. Indeed, Anna comes to the intelligence unit as a complete innocent. She knows neither how to make a cup of tea nor of the existence of electricity bills. She sleeps with a teddy bear. At nineteen her idealism, like her patriotism, is absolutely untested.

Licking Hitler traces Anna's movement from innocence through experience to disillusionment and the brink of despair. Entirely cut off from her loving family, Anna can accept Archie's drunken brutality but not his denial of her as a person. Fennel even admits that Anna's uncle is angry because she has been assigned to work for a savage like Maclean.

Archie's final betrayal of Anna is cut from the same fabric as his inflammatory scripts. His accusations, carefully scripted for delivery by Langley, are as cunning as they are menacing: "You have tried unsuccessfully to get him to sleep with you. Please. There is the question of legality—your age. Also Maclean knows something of your background, your family, how little you know of the world, and felt to take advantage would be indefensible. And he has come to feel that the pressure is now intolerable and rather than have to upset you in person, he has asked me to request you to resign" (123). Yet Archie's consummate hypocrisy does not completely eclipse Anna's love. Years later Anna writes to him and, in doing so, sums up a recurrent theme in Hare's plays: "Over the years I have been watching the steady impoverishment of the people's ideals, their loss of faith, the lying, the daily inveterate lying, the thirty-year-old deep corrosive national habit of lying, and I have remembered you. I have remembered the one lie you told to make me go away. And I now at last have come to understand why you told it. . . . For thirty years you have been the beat of my heart" (128). Unable to cash in on her experiences as the others do, Anna makes a separate peace that rejects Archie's war on class and goodness by going off to live with an unwed mother in Wales.

Themes and Images   The setting of *Licking Hitler,* both in place and in time, is crucial. The play begins in the spring of 1941. On 10–11 May two events transpired: Rudolf Hess arrived in Scotland, presumably to garner British support for Germany's war against Russia, and London sustained a major attack in the Blitz (the last for three years) that damaged the House of Commons.

The isolation of these characters in an English country manor is especially important. Left to their own devices, like the young boys in William Golding's *Lord of the Flies,* they invent a social dynamic based on raw power and its exercise. Its billiard room converted into the broadcast studio, the estate itself is emblematic of the lost splendor of the empire. Quartered in the country house, the staff dines on exquisite china amid beautiful landscapes. But their main course at dinner consists of meat by-products that "squish" when sliced, and even tea is rationed. Consistently Hare juxtaposes the deprivation of their basic needs and the opulence of their surroundings. As time passes, not only material needs but spiritual and emotional ones go unsatisfied. Visually, Hare effectively conveys images of isolation, not only of the group but especially of Anna. When, for example, Eileen learns of her brother's death in combat, she is packed off to vent her emotions in solitude. Herr Jungke is daily driven back to the internment camp where he is kept in solitary confinement because of security regulations.

The secrecy of the black propagandists directly carries over into their personal lives. Like *The Great Exhibition, Licking Hitler* is divided into public and private lives, realized technically through crosscutting. Archie's denial of any sexual relationship with Anna attempts to separate the personal and the public absolutely. Skilled in slander, Archie uses the identical technique he uses against his country's enemies to smear her reputation and have her dismissed. The country estate becomes a different battleground for Archie—one where the class war is fought on distinctly intimate terms.

Sources *Licking Hitler* had its genesis in Hare's chance meeting of Sefton Delmar. Delmar's *Black Boomerang,* an autobiographical account of black propaganda radio broadcasts during World War II, provides many of the most incredible incidents in *Licking Hitler.* Delmar created the character of Gustav Siegfried Eins—Der Chef—an outspoken German patriot who is the model for Hare's Otto. Hare borrows nearly the exact dates of Der Chef's broadcasts, from just after Rudolph Hess's arrival in Scotland on 11 May 1941 until Der Chef's supposed death in October 1943, as the time frame for *Licking Hitler.*

The caustic, inflammatory language of the broadcast is by no means exaggerated. Delmar's Der Chef actually described Hess's defection in this way: "He loses his head completely, packs himself a satchel full of hormone pills and a white flag, and flies off to throw himself and us on the mercy of that flat-footed bastard of a drunken Jew Churchill."[6] Der Chef did indeed broadcast accounts that Slavic blood supposedly contaminated with venereal diseases was used for transfusions. Agents did steam open the mail from Germans to Americans to cull gossip that might titillate listeners. The young burgomaster of Cologne was the target of Der Chef's tales of perversion and indulgence.

Perhaps the most disturbing thing about *Black Boomerang* is neither the name-dropping nor Delmar's sense of self-importance, but the glee with which Delmar cultivates perverse, incendiary stories. Also telling are the mistakes, gaffes, and blunders of Der Chef and his cronies. The final broadcast, for instance, was mistakenly aired twice. No one who heard both transmissions could have doubted they were black propaganda.

The activities described in those memoirs speak to Hare "not just of England then but of England now"[7]—an indication that Hare sees England as still engaged in vicious efforts to fight corruption with corruption. As in other works, Hare shows that very proximity of the hatred and filth of the broadcasts taints the lives of those who create it.

Dreams of Leaving

Since 1968, the time of *How Brophy Made Good,* social and political unrest in Britian has become more subdued but no less desperate.

Indeed, many of Hare's characters of the late 1970s and 1980s lead lives of what Thoreau called "quiet desperation." In *Dreams of Leaving,* among his least political of plays, Hare looks back to the irredeemable innocence and idealism of the early 1970s through the eyes of his narrator, a man now rooted in material comfort and hypocrisy. And, like many of Hare's characters, William Cofax in *Dreams of Leaving* owes the former to the latter.

Two years before the broadcast of *Dreams of Leaving* in 1979, Hare characterized his age and his plays in this way: "We are living through a great, groaning, yawling festival of change—but because this is England it is not always seen on the streets. In my view it is seen in the extraordinary intensity of peoples' [sic] personal despair, and it is to that despair that as a historical writer I choose to address myself."[8] The second of Hare's published scripts for television, *Dreams of Leaving* might provide the title for many of his plays. Once again Hare presents maturity as a choice between madness and compromise.

Dreams of Leaving is narrated by William Cofax, a journalist who comes to London from the provinces in 1971, nine years before the play was first broadcast. In voice-over William recalls the innocent and naive ideals he brought to Fleet Street. Shortly after arriving in London, William meets Caroline, whom he first sees in the company of a drug dealer. As he admits, Caroline has a strange effect on him: "I was never myself with her."[9] *Dreams of Leaving* presents William's memories of their fragmented, unrealized relationship.

Caroline mysteriously drifts in and out of William's life and through a series of careers. Baffled by Caroline, William hears of her promiscuity from other men but he himself sees her only rarely. Each time she comes to the brink of sleeping with him, she vanishes without explanation or trace. William interviews Caroline at work in a small art gallery; they return to his flat; but as they undress an emergency summons Caroline back to work. When William calls her a week later, she rebuffs him.

He later finds her working as the publicity agent for a rock group. Caroline tells him of her new interests and shows him a series of photographs of women in brothels she has taken. Again, she goes home with him only to refuse a sexual relationship with him by announcing that she is in love with him.

Meanwhile William's ideals about journalism quickly fade. His paper reports life "given over to royalty and dogs" (32). At a staff meeting, he chides his fellow reporters: "We know in our hearts what we produce is poor" (32). Only the possibility of pleasing Caroline seems to inspire William. But when he shows her work of which he is especially proud, she dismisses him as spoiled and self-seeking.

Caroline's next career is as a dancer. When William tracks her down, she says he is the only one she has ever loved, but she soon moves in with another man. Seeing this as yet another betrayal, William becomes deliberately promiscuous himself, as if intent on punishing other women for Caroline's treatment of him or, perhaps, in imitation of her.

Again Caroline disappears. William learns that she has starved herself to the point where she now hallucinates. He visits her mother, an eminently dislikable person, and eventually finds Caroline in a mental institution. There he apologizes to her: "I'm sorry. I feel . . . I let you down badly. I should have seen you earlier" (39). But the damage Caroline has suffered, emotional as well as physiological, is irreversible. Seeing her helpless condition in the sanitarium, William finally feels free of any commitment to her. As William leaves the psychiatric hospital he expresses relief: "I was grateful . . . Thank God she was mad" (39).

The final scenes show William in a conventional suburban existence. In a cozy home with his son and daughter, William admits little possibility of real happiness in his "open marriage" with his wife Laura. His life is thoroughly comfortable and completely hypocritical. With Caroline gone from his life, his ideals exist only in memory.

Characters Like Susan Traherne, Caroline can separate sex and love completely; her relationship with William, whether love or friendship, recalls Jenny's with Molloy in *Knuckle*—both are based on the exclusion of sex. Like Karen in *Wetherby,* Caroline seems to be missing a faculty—specifically an emotional capacity that would admit the possibility of love coupled with sex. While she does relate her experiences to William, her sexual exploits in particular, she is unresponsive to his emotional or sexual needs. She consistently refuses both sex and a real emotional relationship with him. While Susan's relationship with Mick represents sex without love, Caroline's relationship with William is supposed to be love without sex.

Caroline prefaces her admission that she loves William by saying "I'm very frightened. I'm in love with you" (26). Caroline and, to a lesser extent, William fear love because it entails not only vulnerability but also commitment. Fearing intimacy coupled with love, let alone vulnerability or commitment, she disciplines herself to independence.

Caroline insists on self-reliance, freedom from commitments to others. While wasting away in withdrawal from the world, "she had some idea of living on her own" (37). In retrospect William reckons that "What I always took to be her self-confidence, now seems a way she had of hiding her fears" (40). Like Susan and Maggie, Caroline has a ferocious desire for independence that drives her to self-inflicted suffering. Her detachment accounts for her mystery, her cachet, but also for her madness.

Caroline's inability to make a commitment appears not only in her personal affairs, but in her work as well. She drifts from one job to the next, from one man to the next, with absolutely no sense of loyalty or satisfaction. She loses her job at the art gallery because she runs off three extra lithographs for herself. She quits the rock group because some work was rejected. She proclaims herself "a very, very good photographer" (24), but never pursues that interest. Unable to reconcile her ideals and reality in either a career or a relationship, Caroline lapses into madness.

William devotes himself to Caroline in a way that recalls the ideals of courtly love. Caroline inspires him and fuels his noblest instincts, but their relationship is never consummated. Caroline attributes that to William's look—"the look that says 'help me.' I'm sorry I can't" (25). In fact, she can neither help him nor sleep with him.

While involved with Caroline, William does take a stand at the newspaper offices by challenging his colleagues: "Why do journalists become cynics? Is it really the things that they see? Isn't it more likely . . . the cause of their unhappiness . . . is something to do with a loss in themselves? I dread a lifetime randomly producing something which we all distrust and despise" (32). That, sadly, is precisely the lifetime that William sees before him and accepts at the end of the play.

William compromises, professionally and privately, without great protestation. A sense of fatality pervades *Dreams of Leaving*. At the outset William says: "Time of course has cemented things over, so this now seems like the inevitable course" (11); at the very end he speculates that had he been wiser, he would have realized the impossibility of Caroline's ever reaching out to him (41). By the end of the play, William has reconciled himself to his loss of Caroline. Gone are the idealism and crusading spirit that are inextricably linked in his memory with youth and the person of Caroline. Without Caroline to remind him of those ideals, William soon drifts into compromise as surely as Caroline lapses into madness.

In *Dreams of Leaving* Hare identifies youth with idealism, naïveté, and hope. Age and experience, however, seem to offer only the choice between madness and compromise. William ends with the painful admission that breaks the facade of easy acceptance: "We have, each and everyone of us, dreams of leaving"—dreams, that is, of lost ideals that cannot survive in the world. William's despair is neither ostentatious nor self-pitying. He simply admits that "Obviously Caroline is much with me" (40) in the same way that Lazar was always much with Susan Traherne.

Images and Themes   The futility and compromise of work is evident in Caroline's always short-lived careers as an art dealer, photographer, publicist, and dancer as well as in William's disgust with Fleet Street hacks. No matter what employment characters find, producing quality work is unimportant, even detrimental to one's success. Stievel, his editor, offers this evaluation of one of William's first articles: "It's fine. It's absolute rubbish. Congratulations. You have the house style" (14). In the very next sequence, Caroline explains how paintings—works of art by Picasso, Bacon, Hockney—are appraised:

> *CAROLINE:*   Well it depends on the size. When we can get hold of one we look in the price book, there's a charge per square foot; we take a tape measure, work it out like that. . . .
>
> *WILLIAM:*   Doesn't quality come into it?
>
> *CAROLINE:*   Of course not. Why should it? That's not our job.
>
> *WILLIAM:*   But if Bacon painted a masterpiece, wouldn't they feel that they had to charge more?
>
> *CAROLINE:*   Good Lord no, what, hell are you mad? Then when he did a bad one, they'd have to charge less.
>
> (16)

Corruption is ubiquitous: brothels flourish, the police accept bribes, journalists pander to the public. Everything can be marketed, honesty or quality have little bearing on marketability.

When Caroline turns to a career as a dancer, she begins to withdraw even further into herself. She tells William: "I'm really pleased. I'd forgotten the discipline" (34). That discipline and withdrawal becomes even more extreme when she abandons dance class and turns to reclusion and starvation. Caroline's literal starvation reduces her weight to

only ninety-eight pounds, brings on hallucinations, and causes irrevoca-
ble damage. Her refusal to allow love and sex to coalesce in her relationship with William is a spiritual starvation. While *Dreams of Leaving*
contains no sanctimonious moral implications about chastity, the casual
sex of both Caroline and William—specifically her refusal to admit the
possibility of a relationship where sex and love might coincide—is
presented as inimical to life itself. It is a form of self-destructive behavior not unlike Maggie's alcoholism or Susan's drug dependence. Like
alcohol and drugs, the denial of emotional needs provides a hardened
exterior to face a world of despair.

Summation

Dreams of Leaving moves away from the historical events that plot the
decline of the empire to the much more intimate analysis of the diminished possibilities for personal relationships that approximates love.
Indeed, love seems to be a remote ideal, held only by the naïve and
innocent—the young William or nineteen-year-old Anna Seaton.

Both works, like *Plenty,* show that honesty and integrity—
professional or personal—are detrimental to success. Those who are
most successful are those who were never burdened with ideals. In
contrast to the successful professional careers of Langley, Fennel, and
Archie, Anna does not achieve success, specifically because of her need
"to live an honest life" (126). Once he successfully contains the memory of Caroline and his idealism, William basks in the material comfort that is the reward of mediocrity. With nothing to overcome in
the road to mediocrity, most of these characters accept compromise as
a natural part of life.

Both in *Dreams of Leaving* and *Licking Hitler* Hare successfully uses
the techniques of television—flashbacks and flashforwards—to contrast
youth and age, innocence and experience. The contrast is essential to
Hare's themes of disillusionment and despair. In his major stage plays
since 1978, Hare has adapted these techniques to the stage.

Chapter Seven

Films

Wetherby

Wetherby is one of the few works by Hare that does not employ a linear progression of time. Governed by memory, dreams, and association, *Wetherby* draws together episodes from the near and the distant past—episodes linked in Jean Traverse's mind by physical intimacy and violent death. The film's expressionistic use of time intersperses flashbacks of Jean's affair with an airman, Jim, in the early 1950s in the unfolding events in the 1980s. Framed by conversations between Stanley Pilborough and Jean in a pub, the film opens as they discuss Nixon's bizarre courtship of his wife, Pat.

At Jean's "perfect Yorkshire farmhouse . . . [the] image of rundown serenity,"[1] Stanley and Marcia Pilborough, Verity and Roger Braithwaite, and John Morgan gather for a dinner party. What transpires when Jean and Morgan go upstairs to investigate a leak in the roof is not, at this point, revealed, but recurrent flashbacks will dwell on it. Morgan embraces Jean; when she resists him, he drags her to the floor. Her clothing ripped, she changes from a skirt into slacks before returning to her guests downstairs.

Jean teaches English literature—Shakespeare in particular. After class one day, Suzie Bannerman, a student, asks if Jean sees any point in her continuing her education. At fifteen, Suzie is not responsive to Jean's ideals concerning education as "a thing in itself, a way of fulfilling your potential, of looking for ways of thinking" (16). As far as Suzie can see, "whatever you do, you seem to end up unemployed" (16).

That evening as Jean sits outside her home, Morgan arrives carrying a brace of pheasant as a gift. Over a cup of tea, Morgan explains that no one invited him to Jean's dinner party. In flashbacks, narrated by Morgan's "confession," he simply appears at the doorstep and is accepted into Jean's house. Jean and her guests all mistakenly assume someone else invited him. Without warning or comment, Morgan takes a revolver from his pocket, puts it in his mouth, and pulls the trigger. That act of desperate violence transforms not only the present and the future, but the past as well. Every detail of Morgan's interaction with Jean and her friends now takes on an added importance. As similarities between Jean's affair with Jim and her encounter with Morgan haunt her, even trivial details become fraught with significance.

The next sequence moves back to 1953, to the young Jean making love to Jim, an RAF mechanic, who decides to accept a posting in Malaya. In her diary that night, Jean writes that she "never knew any such happiness was possible at all" (24).

Hare has now, only fifteen minutes into the film, established a recent as well as distant past through flashbacks—the first shows Jean's encounter with John Morgan; the second her affair with Jim. A third man enters Jean's present life in the person of a police detective, Mike Langdon, who arrives to investigate Morgan's death. It is easy enough for the police to accept that Morgan killed himself because he was depressed; the more difficult question is why he chose to commit suicide in front of Jean. Langdon visits Jean, who has been left to clean up the bloody mess, and tells her that Morgan was a doctoral student at the University of Essex who had come to Wetherby to do research at the British Library Lending Division. Marcia, who works at the library, refused his request to borrow a book because he did not have the proper credentials.

Jean's friendship with Marcia triggers another flashback to 1953 as Jean confides to Marcia her romance with Jim; from that, the film moves forward to their friendship thirty years on, and to a picture of Jean's house that Marcia brought as a gift to the dinner party.

As Jean tries to relax in a bath after Langdon's visit, we see Morgan's train trip to and arrival in Wetherby. Standing at the window of his rented room holding his pistol, Morgan is a sniper in search of a target. The parallel between Jean and Langdon is developed through a later matching shot of Langdon in his bath, also pondering Morgan's case.

The morning after Morgan's suicide Marcia and Stanley visit Jean to console her. When Marcia asks Jean if Morgan might have been offended in some way, Jean says only that she thinks Morgan chose to kill himself in front of her because they shared "a feeling for solitude" (36). This statement triggers Jean's recollection of meeting Jim's parents, who are remarkably unresponsive to Jean's plans to study at university while Jim serves in Malaya. Jean's isolation in that situation is not only the link between herself and Morgan, but between present and past as well.

Drawn into the mystery of Morgan's suicide and Jean's loneliness, Langdon plans to visit Jean, bringing with him a gift of flowers that a woman officer reminds him is unnecessary. By crosscutting Jean's affair with Jim, her encounter with Morgan, and her visits from Langdon, Hare portrays Jean's restraint, her self-control, and her isolation.

Thinking she best keep herself busy, Jean goes in to teach. When she accidentally discovers Suzie kissing a boy, Jean simply turns and walks away. That evening Jean discovers Karen, Morgan's girlfriend, on her doorstep. Karen explains that she knew Morgan only casually: she went to two films with Morgan, then he started pestering her. Jean takes Karen in, sets her up with a television, but can discover no basis of communication with her. Langdon, in fact, had suggested that Karen visit Jean. On a rainy night in Leeds, Jean happens to encounter Langdon and his live-in girlfriend, Chrissie, in a Chinese restaurant. As Langdon drives her home, Jean explains that Karen, with whom Morgan was obsessed, is still staying with her. Langdon walks Jean inside her house, sees Karen sleeping soundly, and stands just where Morgan stood when he attacked Jean. Now he, too, figures in Jean's association of Morgan and Jim.

The flashbacks concerning Morgan's life move closer to the time of his suicide. After his encounter with Marcia at the library, he waits for her, stalks her in the parking lot, and stands outside her home watching her through the window. But at a jumble sale Morgan, staring at Jean, "has found what he is looking for" (60)—the object for his violence.

Jean brings Karen with her to a school play, a production of *A Man for All Seasons* that she has directed. When a man asks Karen a simple question, she drops her drink and screams at the man to leave her alone. Hare crosscuts from the confrontation between Karen and the man to the encounter between Morgan and Karen. Morgan breaks in to Karen's room at the university, wrestles her to the floor and screams "I want some feeling! I want some contact! I want you fucking near me!" (65). Karen resents any inquisitiveness, any attempts to establish a personal relationship: she rejects Morgan's insistent pleas just as she resists the parent's question and Jean's curiosity. Jean is no more successful in reaching Karen. Despite Jean's kindness and generosity, Karen walks out on Jean, leveling a bitter accusation that Jean precipitated Morgan's suicide.

The pacing of the film, especially in the final third, is especially effective. The crosscutting moves closer toward Jean's encounter with Morgan, Jim's murder in Malaya, and Langdon's discovery of Jean's secret. Karen's accusation again takes Jean back to her romance with Jim. Meanwhile, Roger Braithwaite visits Langdon with the clue to solving the mystery of Morgan: when Jean came back downstairs at the dinner party, she had changed her clothes. Langdon realizes that Jean was somehow personally involved with Morgan. Almost simultaneously, Langdon discovers that Chrissie has left him. He goes to Jean and tries to elicit an admission from her. In each other's arms they discover that they, too, share a feeling for solitude. The film ends where it began: with Stanley and Jean in the pub where they raise a toast "To all our escapes."

Themes and Images   One of the questions that plagues Jean is whether she caused or contributed to the suicide of John Morgan. Marcia, Jean's best friend, asks: "Does anyone know why he did it? And why on earth did he choose to come and do it to you?" (35). Chrissie, Langdon's girlfriend, suggests that Jean might have done "something to provoke" (46) Morgan. Karen lashes out at Jean in an accusatory, "If it wasn't an accident, I'd love to know what *you* did" (67). Long after the completion of his official investigation, Langdon visits Jean and asks her "What happened? Was it your fault?" (73).

For Jean, the more important and complex question lies in her feelings of guilt about Jim's death, not Morgan's. Had Jean admitted that she loved and needed Jim, he would not have gone to Malaya and died. But this sense of guilt has more to do with emotional honesty than with moral failure. Jean wanted Jim to do what *he* wanted to do. She could in no way foresee his murder, but has had to live with its consequences for all of her adult life.

When Marcia asks why Morgan chose Jean as the witness to his suicide, Jean replies that "the lonely recognize the lonely" (35). Equally important is the emotional reserve that ties together the various plots and subplots in *Wetherby*. In the lives of Jean and her friends, Langdon, and Karen the inability to articulate emotional needs is the common bond and, most likely, the key to understanding Morgan's suicide.

Emotional detachment and repression pervade *Wetherby*. The only sequence concerning Morgan and Karen, presented in flashback, directly parallels the encounter between Morgan and Jean: Karen and Jean rebuff Morgan under very similar circumstances. As Morgan menacingly embraces Jean he tells her: "You're in trouble. . . . You're lonely. . . . All that hope coming out of you. All that cheerful resolution. All that wonderful enlightenment. For what? For nothing" (87).

In one sense Jean's cheerfulness is very real. Her devotion to her students, the time she spends counseling Suzie, the care she takes in directing the school play are all indicative of a purpose she has found in life. Yet none of these can replace the physical intimacy and happiness that she once shared with Jim.

A sense of decorum and conventionality weighs heavily on these characters. Roger describes the necessity of such barriers. "Logic also tells you that there must be constraints, and that if everyone went round saying what they truly feel, the result would be barbarism" (49). The celebrated British manners pervade the play and account for the emotional reticence of the characters. When Stanley candidly inquires about Morgan at Jean's dinner, Marcia upbraids him: "Stanley, don't be rude" (48). Thinking that he is a friend of Marcia, Jean readily accepts Morgan into her home. Later, after Karen arrives, Jean finds it impossible to ask her to leave although Karen clearly makes Jean's life miserable.

The younger characters share a profound sense of futility and hopelessness. Suzie tells Jean that she sees no point in continuing her education because of the slim-to-nil prospects of a decent job. Karen advances this sense of futility to an emotional level where it affects all personal relations: "You make an effort, you try to be nice, try to do anything . . . you just get your head chopped off. Why try?" (66). And near the end of the film, when we finally see the confrontation between Morgan and Jean, Morgan's most menacing accusation against Jean doubts even the possibility of Jean's happiness: "You know it's for nothing. Don't tell me that cheerfulness is real" (87).

The characters of Jean's generation have a variety of ways in which they give meaning to their lives. Together they enjoy camaraderie. Some, like Jean, find meaning through work. Others, like Roger, find meaning in hobbies. But more characteristic are these dreams of leaving that appear in each character of every generation.

Landscape and Setting Wetherby is an actual town in the northeast of England, near Leeds, site of the British Library Lending Division. The drab industrial landscape of Leeds establishes an effective contrast with Jean's cottage. In Leeds Jean glimpses a particularly chilling scene of children playing around a bonfire, smashing sticks and screaming, which shows how inhospitable the modern urban environment is.[2] Jean's cottage also stands in contrast to the modern educational facilities—the University of Essex and the BLLD—barren fortresses of security and paranoia that offer Morgan and Karen little respite from the emotional sterility of their lives. A montage of the University of Essex is described in this way: "The tower block at the University of Essex stands gaunt against the sky. More like a housing estate than a university. . . . A gulch of tower blocks. They stand, lined up, sinister, desolated. Scraps of paper blow down between them. A scene more like urban desolation than a university. Concrete stanchions, deserted. . . . An empty lift automatically opens its doors. Inside it is painted blue. Someone has scrawled, 'Fuck you All' " (63–64). In such a hostile environment, the desperation and loneliness of these characters, epitomized by Morgan's suicide, seem almost inevitable.

Characters   Hare effectively contrasts the younger characters—Morgan and Karen—and those nearer to Jean's (and Hare's) own age. Langdon characterizes Morgan as having "a central disfiguring blankness" (28). The arrival of a new young girl, "not a person, not a real person" (12), at work evokes this tirade from Marcia: "I look at the young—truly—and I am mystified. Want nothing. Need nothing. Have no ambitions. Get married, have children, get a mortgage. A hundred thousand years of human evolution, brontosaurus, tyrannosaurus, man. And the sum ambition? Two-up two-down in the West Riding of Yorkshire, on a custom-built estate of brick and glass" (12). Karen also fits Marcia's description of the young. After several days of trying to find some common ground with Karen, Jean tells Langdon "it's as if she's missing a faculty" (55). Karen readily loses herself and buries whatever anguish she feels over Morgan's death simply by watching television. Not only does Jean fail to elicit any sign of grief, but Karen resents any effort—by Morgan, Jean, or the man—to make contact with her. This younger generation, one that recalls the inarticulate desolation of Lesley, the teenager in *Lay By,* finds even the simplest, most basic human contact an unlikely prospect. Hare's treatment of Karen is especially damning because, as in *Teeth 'n' Smiles,* youth might be expected to offer an alternative to the deadened sensibilities of middle age, yet it clearly does not.

Jean's youth was quite unlike that of Karen and the young girl Marcia describes. Jean's affair with Jim establishes a remarkable contrast with present-day events because of its passion and happiness, its comparative openness and directness. Although the young Jean says "with him I can't talk. With him I can't say anything I feel" (69), she believed that she and Jim could enjoy a commitment to each other despite parental objections, separation, and "a gulf" (69) between them.

The characters of Jean's generation have at least their friendships; those between Jean and Stanley and Jean and Marcia certainly seem genuine enough. Jean's dinner party is honestly convival, but her generation is not without its hypocrisy and loneliness. Marital squabbles and infidelities punctuate their lives. When Verity flairs up against her husband Roger at Jean's dinner party, Stanley describes them as "warring parties" (50). Roger casually reveals to Marcia that he went on vacation not with Verity but with a woman who teaches home economics. Marcia harangues Stanley about drinking too much. Stanley tells Jean "If you're frightened of loneliness, never get married" (36).

Sources   The shocking episode of *Wetherby,* Morgan's suicide, evokes a nearly identical image at the beginning of Christopher Hampton's *The Philanthropist.* There, too, ten minutes into the work a character puts a revolver in his mouth and pulls the trigger. Hare, who knew Hampton since boyhood, surprisingly says that the similarity is pure coincidence.

Hare describes *Wetherby* as his "privet-hedge film. It's about what it's like to be brought up in suburban respectability, in which any kind of emotional outgoingness is frowned upon."[3]

Several reviewers pointed out a comparison between *Wetherby* and the plays of Harold Pinter, particularly in the silences—sometimes cryptic, sometimes menacing—that punctuate the film. Perhaps more to the point is that the silences recall the laconic dialogue of film noir. Although filmed in color, *Wetherby* is dominated by gray, subdued colors and has the underpinning of a mystery/detective investigator. Langdon is an admirable and astute investigator, not only because he is kind, but because he is insightful. Unlike Jean's closest friends, he discovers the emotional reality underlying her placid reserve and comforts her. Perhaps even more clearly than Curly in *Knuckle,* Langdon recalls the code and compassion of Ross Macdonald's Lew Archer. (Like Archer, Langdon leaves the police force but never forsakes his code.)

Critical Acclaim   Critical response to *Wetherby* was extremely varied. British critics were, in general, more responsive to it than Americans, some of whom seemed positively baffled by the film. Writing in *Time* Richard Corliss complained, "European in form, English in its turbid psychological climate, the film could have been called *Last Year at Weatherbad.*"[4] Rex Reed was obtuse in dismissing the film: "It takes a ponderous amount of time for the fragments of this incoherent story to come together, and even when they do, the results are irritating, unsatisfying, and contentious."[5]

David Sterritt, writing in the *Christian Science Monitor,* was far more astute in observing that "Hare's view of human nature is sensitive enough to insist that even the smallest and most commonplace lives are teeming with significance and interest, if we just bother to look. . . . it's a promising debut film from a man associated with the theatre until now."[6] Likewise, Andrew Sarris, in the *Village Voice,* acclaimed the film as "a morbidly fascinating, brilliantly acted pscyhosociological mystery."[7]

Not all of the British responses were positive. *Sight and Sound* called it "an apology for a thriller which has no other narrative thrust to sustain an audience."[8] More typical of the British reviews, however, was *Monthly Film Bulletin,* the publication of the British Film Institute, which also carried an interview with Hare with its very favorable review of the film.

Film Adaptation of *Plenty*

The film adaptation of *Plenty* featured Meryl Streep in place of Kate Nelligan, who appeared as Susan Traherne both in the London and New York productions and to whom the play is dedicated. Fred Schepisi directed Hare's own screen adaptation.

During the three-week rehearsal period that preceded the filming, Hare, at Streep's urging, restored "big chunks"[9] from the stage play that he had originally cut. The result is a film that, while not directed by Hare, is uncommonly faithful to the spirit of the stage play.

With the cryptic first scene of the play cut, the film is framed, in the manner of *Wetherby,* by episodes set in France when Susan was seventeen. Many of the episodes only briefly alluded to in the play—Susan's employment at a shipping office, in the civil service, and in advertising—are filmed to underscore the pointlessness and tedium of her work. Visually the film is effective in drawing stark contrasts between the austerity of British life in the late forties and fifties and the opulence of the diplomatic environments. The set decoration and cinematography convey the sense of material plenty in Susan's Knightsbridge home and the diplomatic world.

One of the sequences added in the film, in which Alice comes to visit Brock and Susan during their posting in Jordan (rather than Iran) in 1961, is a welcomed thematic and visual amplification of the stage play.

Susan's withdrawal from life and dependence upon drugs are such that she barely pauses to greet Alice. Against a stark, parched landscape, Susan and Brock shield themselves from the intrusions of any native culture. They drive Alice to look at the ruins of an amphitheater, but remain ensconced in their chauffeur-driven Jaguar. When Alice challenges the wisdom of keeping Susan sedated and isolated, Brock responds, "I don't like the life people live in London. All that money does nobody good. It rots them. It does untold damage, as well you know. Life becomes excitable, flashy, decadent, frenzied, diseased. Here there is peace and quiet—a level way of living. I think you'll find it suits Susan very well."[10] Even while sedated, however, Susan always keeps with her the pair of cuff links Lazar left in her bedroom during the war.

The film received generally positive reviews. Reviewers touched upon the ambivalence toward and contradictions within the character of Susan Traherne. Reviewers also consistently praised the acting, especially in the supporting roles of Alice (Tracey Ullman), Brock (Charles Dance), Charleson (Ian McKellan), and Darwin (John Gielgud). Some challenged the replacement of Kate Nelligan, yet no one doubted that Streep's talent and celebrity increased audience size.

Hare's Place among British Filmmakers in the 1980s

Since the early 1980s the British film industry has enjoyed a renaissance owing partially to the formation of British production companies like Hand-Made Films (cofounded in 1978 by George Harrison and Denis O'Brien), Nelson Entertainment, Goldcrest, and Film Four International. While there has never been any paucity of British actors, these and other companies have produced the work of a new generation of British directors, including Bill Forsyth (*Gregory's Girl* [1981], *Local Hero* [1983]), Peter Greenaway (*The Draughtman's Contract* [1982], *Drowning by Numbers* [1988]), and Stephen Frears (who directed Hare's *Saigon* for Thames Television and *My Beautiful Laundrette* [1985], *Sammy and Rosie Get Laid* [1987], and *Prick Up Your Ears* [1987]). Given the well-established British directors (like John Boorman and Lindsay Anderson), the former members of Monty Python (Terry Gilliam and Terry Jones), and the emergence of theatrical directors like Hare and Richard Eyre, there is now an explosion of British filmmakers directing British actors in British scripts about British themes.

Plenty, although produced by an American company (Twentieth Century Fox) and directed by an Australian (Fred Schepisi), contains an almost prescient exploration of the theme that dominates many recent British films: the postcolonial decline of Britain. In films as diverse in style and substance as *The Shooting Party* (1984), *Brazil* (1985), *A Month in the Country* (1988), *Pascali's Island* (1988), and *A Passage to India* (1984), filmmakers dwell on the decline of the British empire, and especially on the implications for those who survive that decline. Many of these films offer a striking contrast between the opulence and splendor of the past (clearly seen in *A Room with a View* [1985], *The Shooting Party, A Handful of Dust* [1988], and *White Mischief* [1987]) and the wasteland that is Thatcher's Britain (e.g., *Sammy and Rosie Get Laid, Sid and Nancy* [1986], and *Mona Lisa* [1986]). The contrast between the wealth of the upper class and the penury of ordinary people is as strong as the contrast between past and present. Moreover, the films that do depict the grandeur of Britain's past usually do so ironically, as if the indulgence of previous generations is a debt—financial, political, or moral—that has now come due. The empire's spoils suggest, as Hare clearly does in *Plenty,* that material prosperity begets spiritual poverty.

The landscape of British films set in the 1980s is often the urban wasteland from which Jean in *Wetherby* takes refuge and that we glimpse on her visit to Leeds. *Sammy and Rosie Get Laid,* for instance, opens with a vista of London's smoldering junk heaps. *Sid and Nancy, The Good Father* (1987), *My Beautiful Laundrette, A Letter to Brezhnev* (1985), and *28 Up* (1985) all graphically depict an environment ravaged by the economic woes of the Great Depression, devastated by World War II and the postwar austerity, and ignored in the bloodletting of the Thatcher government. The prosperity of the sixties and early seventies goes virtually unseen and unfelt. What remain are hopelessness and despair not simply in the economic future, but in any sort of future. In such worlds, the police, and in retrospect most people, find the violence and desperation of Morgan's suicide unsurprising.

The themes and character types of *Wetherby* also appear in films like *84 Charing Cross Road* (1987; written by an American, Helen Hanff), *The Lonely Passion of Judith Hearne* (1988; based on Brian Moore's novel), and *Turtle Diary* (1985). In each a middle-aged person, drained by years of sexual reticence and conformity to a rigid decorum, almost miraculously discovers an unlikely romance. More typically passion and romance seem unlikely except among homosexuals, who—as in *Maurice* (1984), *Another Country* (1984; based on Julian Mitchell's 1982 stage play), *Prick Up Your Ears,* and *My Beautiful Laundrette*—retain much of their vitality. When sexuality is not associated with prostitution, as it often is (e.g., *Mona Lisa, Personal Services* [1987], *Dance with a Stranger* [1984], *Prayer for the Dying* [1987]), or with perversion (witness *White Mischief*), it is often imported by Americans as in *Sid and Nancy, A Fish Called Wanda* (1988), and *Stormy Monday* (1988).

Chapter Eight
Global Visions

While most of Hare's plays before 1980 focus on Britain, since then his plays take on a larger scope. *A Map of the World, Saigon: Year of the Cat, The Bay at Nice,* and *Wrecked Eggs* consciously eschew the British setting and instead offer a global vision. Populated by Americans, Russians, Indians, and Africans, as well as Britons, these plays counterpoint the most intimate choices—ones dealing with sex, marriage, and family—with international situations. And while Hare chooses global contexts for these works, he maintains, even intensifies, his focus on the personal lives of his characters.

A Map of the World

In a lounge of a Bombay hotel Stephen Andrews, a young British reporter, unsuccessfully tries to order a drink. He and Elaine le Fanu, a black American journalist, are in Bombay to cover a UNESCO conference on poverty in the third world. The conference's keynote speaker, Victor Mehta, an Indian-born novelist of worldwide repute who lives in Shropshire, soon joins them and has no trouble securing drinks for them all. The conversation between Mehta and Stephen quickly turns into an ideological spat over topics as diverse as homosexuality, third world poverty, and feminism. Declaiming the articles of his faith (e.g., "All old civilizations are superior to younger ones"[1]), Mehta is hardly amenable to any real discussion of his ideas; for him, they are irrefutable.

Mehta invites Elaine to dine with him, a New Delhi professor, and an American jazz violinist, Peggy Whitton. Stephen dislikes Mehta for many reasons. He despises Mehta's "desperately mimicking the manners of a country [England] that died—died in its heart—over thirty, forty, fifty years ago" (168). He rejects Mehta's smug conservatism and loathes the readiness with which Mehta presumes to understand (and to dismiss) liberal opinions. And, perhaps most important, he resents the fact that Mehta has apparently stolen his date, Peggy Whitton.

As Angelis, a film director, and technicians emerge from the shadows, the audience realizes that what has transpired to this point is a scene from a film based on a novel by Mehta. The appearance of the director marks the first of several interruptions in the story of what happened in Bombay. All these interruptions address the relationship between art and reality by examining the fidelity of the film to Mehta's novel and of his novel to actual experience. The "real live" Peggy, for example, tells Angelis: "You've quite destroyed Victor's writing" (172). The actors who seemed so sincere in character a moment before now squabble over details and acrimoniously insult one another. Life and art appear irreconcilable because each individual is wedded to a single perspective, his or her own understanding of events.

Seamlessly, the action fades back into the film script as Martinson, a conference organizer, confronts Mehta with a statement about the relationship between fiction and politics. M. M'Bengue, a delegate from Senegal who helped Stephen draft the statement, argues that Mehta must read the statement because the Western world sees events in the third world only in its own terms: governments are viewed as pro-Western or pro-Soviet. M'Bengue and Stephen demand that Mehta acknowledge the distortions in his writing—distortions even more severe in Mehta's work than in most Western writing because not only is it fiction, but comic fiction. Despite Peggy's prompting, Mehta wants nothing to do with the statement and claims he is the victim of "moral blackmail of the Third World [and] now . . . sexual blackmail" (181) by Peggy. Mehta agrees to negotiate the statement's wording only because he has spent the previous night with Peggy, but when he learns that Stephen drafted the statement, he categorically refuses to read it and storms out. With Elaine as her "witness," Peggy tells Stephen that both he and Mehta have behaved stupidly and proposes a debate between them with Elaine as the adjudicator and herself as the winner's prize.

Act 2 begins with the actors passing time before the rehearsals begin again. The actor playing Martinson works a crossword puzzle and casually asks Elaine for a seven-letter word beginning with "Z": " 'It's the plague of the earth' " (196). Elaine's flippant answer, "Zionism," triggers Martinson's spirited defense of Israel. He quotes Jean-Paul Sartre, asks how she could say something so callous, and demands to know if Elaine really thinks of Zionism as evil. Elaine says she simply guessed at an answer that would fit. M'Bengue finally notices that the answer begins not with "Z" but with "S" and comes up with the true answer: "Slavery." By the time Angelis arrives a rumor has swept through the company: Peggy was so infuriated with the rehearsal that she has persuaded Mehta to file a lawsuit to halt the film's production. The rehearsal of an intimate encounter between Peggy and Mehta leaves the actress Peggy on the verge of tears as she realizes how casually and stupidly Peggy (the character) offered herself as the winner's prize when all she wants is Mehta. Unexpectedly, the events of Peggy's story carry over directly into the actress's life, just as they did both in Peggy's own life and in her outrage over Angelis's treatment of Mehta's novel.

When Stephen and Mehta meet to set out the terms for their debate the next day, another confrontation quickly develops. Convinced he will win because his views are "unarguably correct" (212), Mehta dismisses Stephen's "peasant-like ideas" (212). Describing the genesis of his convictions through his own personal experience, Mehta concludes "that in this universe of idiocy, the only thing we may rely on is the lone voice—the lone voice of the writer—who speaks only when he has something to say. . . . Mankind has one enemy only and it is not poverty. It is self-deception" (215). Rather than challenging Mehta's ideas, Stephen denounces Mehta as capable only of jealousy and lust, and asserts: "If I am to win, I must attack the man. I am arguing that tomorrow you must go out and denounce your own fiction, because it will be your last remaining chance to rejoin the human race" (216). He accuses Mehta of accepting hopelessness and projecting his own despair in his novels. Without apologizing for his ideals, Stephen rejects Peggy's terms for the debate and announces he will leave Bombay that evening. In effect, however, the debate has just taken place and Stephen has won.

The arrival of the "real life" Mehta interrupts this scene. Shocked by Stephen's death in a train accident, Mehta left the conference to claim Stephen's body and was denounced as a fascist and a charlatan. While others use Stephen's death to their own ends, Mehta chooses silence in "memory of Stephen" (224). In the closing lines of the play Mehta speaks of his respect for his son's idealism: "This feeling, finally, that we may change things—this is at the centre of everything we are. Lose that . . . lose that, lose everything" (228).

Characters   Mehta precisely summarizes Hare's treatment of the principal characters in *A Map of the World:* "Each of the characters is forced to examine the values of his or her life. . . . The novelist is accused of dalliance and asked to put a value on what he has seen as a passing affair. The actress questions her easy promiscuity and is made to realize adulthood will involve choice. And Stephen, the journalist, assumes the confidence of his own beliefs" (222). In Bombay, Mehta, Peggy, and Stephen all experience epiphanies that transform their character.

The three principal characters are molded by their own experience, background, and nationality. Just as Hare shows no reluctance in delineating a British national character, he aggressively defines Peggy in distinctly American terms. Peggy says that in America the "only philosophy you'll ever encounter is the philosophy of making money" (207). And she tells Mehta: "When an Englishman has an emotion, his first instinct is to repress it. When an American has an emotion, his first instinct [is to] express it" (206). Like the Americans in *Wrecked Eggs,* Peggy is candid, pragmatic, and direct.

By contrast, Mehta was born in a small Indian village. He immigrated to Britain where he was initially disillusioned: "I went to London, to the university there, to the country where once medicine, education, and law had been practised *sans pareil,* and found instead a country now full of sloth and complacency . . . a deceitful, inward-looking ruling class blundering by its racialism and stupidity into Suez" (213). Hare's own view of Mehta is that "he becomes fastidious about ideas. Smelling a bad idea is like smelling a dirty pair of socks. Horrid, vulgar ideas! He has a little portmanteau of attitudes he develops and then applies to every situation. He misses out on the sheer richness and variety of life. In *Map of the World* I'm trying to say that no intellectual will ever be able to organize the world in the way he wants to organize it."[2] In politics and background, Mehta is loosely modeled on V. S. Naipaul, the Trindad-born novelist and essayist whose works often deal with the relationship between the first and third worlds. Mehta is far less sympathetic to the plight of the third world than is Stephen, who was born into the comfort and privilege of white British life.

Stephen's death forces Mehta to reassess the validity of the accusation that he and his works are filled with disillusionment and despair; that reassessment, in turn, precipitates Mehta's transformation. Mehta does rejoin the human race and recover his lost idealism, but not through any logical or systematic process. He and Peggy are brought together, not just in a passing dalliance, but in a much more profound relationship because of Stephen's death. As critic Benedict Nightingale wrote, "Stephen's arguments and demise combine magically to convert Mehta from a detached jokesmith into someone prepared to commit himself."[3] Peggy is similarly transformed by Stephen. She abandons the casual sexual relations that first brought her to Mehta's bed and marries him. Like Mehta, she shows a fierce loyalty to the memory of Stephen.

The transformation of Stephen is no less important. Heeding Elaine's advice, he tells Peggy: "For years I've apologized. A shambler, a neurotic, I've accepted the picture the world has of an idealist as a man who is necessarily a clown. No shortage of people to tell him he's a fool. And we accept this picture. Yes, we betray our instincts. We betray them because we're embarrassed, and we've lost our conviction that we can make what's best in us prevail" (220). Stephen's decision to reject Peggy's terms for the debate and to leave the conference mark his transformation from shambler to unapologetic idealist.

Structure   The rehearsals, film, and novel all focus on the relationship between Mehta and Stephen. Simultaneously, that story is a love story, an intellectual debate, and an account of the transformations of Mehta, Peggy, and Stephen. Hare's structural technique is to overlap the five scenes reenacting Mehta's story with five scenes dealing with the rehearsals for the film. That scenes flow directly into one another heightens the awareness that what we are seeing is not real life, but a dramatization. Thematically, the technique ideally reflects one of Mehta's (and Hare's) fundamental observations: the difficulty if not impossibility of seeing events from someone else's perspective. Once Angelis and his staff emerge from the shadows, they focus on make-up, lighting, props, setting, impending lawsuits—the technical concerns of filmmakers. At least momentarily they must suspend their interest in Mehta's story and focus exclusively on its effective telling. Conversely, while in character, the actors are absorbed by their rendering of the action and do not concern themselves with the technical details. Depending on one's perspective, the relative importance and even meaning of events can change completely. For Mehta and Peggy, who both were transformed by the events in Bombay, the contrast between reality and art is downright painful.

The counterpoint established by the overlapping of scenes produces a strong sense of irony. At the end of act 1, for instance, as Peggy triumphantly announces Mehta's acceptance of the terms of debate, Angelis immediately undercuts her by announcing his boredom and calling for lunch. The technique is also appropriate in contrasting what characters were before Stephen's death and what they have since become. As in the flashbacks in *Plenty* and *Wetherby,* characters are not what they were. Nor do these characters necessarily have any similarity with the actors who portray them. But when the actress playing Peggy breaks down, the audience sees one instance in which art carries over into life. One source of unity in the play pivots on this interaction: the relationship between art and reality links Mehta's autobiographical novel and the rehearsals, and is at the very heart of what is perhaps Hare's most political play since *Fanshen*.

Politics Throughout *A Map of the World* Hare focuses on the impossibility of separating the individual from his ideology. The Senegalese delegate M'Bengue argues that Western writers—journalists and novelists alike—can only see events in the third world from a Western perspective. As M'Bengue says of the severe terms of a loan he secures for his country: "You throw us a lifeline. The lifeline is in the shape of a noose" (227). Similarly, Mehta's arguments are littered with ad hominem anecdotes about world leaders he disdains: Castro's appearance as an extra in an Esther Williams movie; Mao Tse-tung's weaknesses in publishing his own poetry and marrying an actress. Stephen most successfully counters Mehta by pointing to the despair in Mehta's own works.

Mehta argues that the United Nations is a failure and a sham: "Instead of sending the Third World doctors and mechanics, we now send them hippies, and Marxist thinkers, and animal conservationists, and ecologists, and wandering fake Zen Buddhist students, who hasten to reassure the illiterate that theirs is a superior life to that of the West" (214). Yet Stephen's refutation of Mehta's ideas focuses on Mehta's own humanity. Not only in its politics but also in its intimacy, Stephen's argument is antithetical to Mehta's logical, measured case. And for every character personal perspectives determine political convictions.

These political questions are further complicated by an underlying debate about the work of artists—novelists, filmmakers, and playwrights. The disclaimer authored by Stephen and M'Bengue states: " 'Fiction, by its very nature, must always be different from fact, so in a way a man who stands before you as a writer of fiction is already halfway towards admitting that a great deal of what he makes up and invents is as much with an eye to entertainment as it is to presenting literal historical truth' " (181). Mehta not only finds the statement unacceptable, he even calls it "Nazi" (181). On another level, the tension between the truth of art and the truth of reality in *A Map of the World* pivots on the autobiographical nature of the novel on which the film is based. "The real Peggy Whitton, on whom Victor Mehta based his great novel" (172), who has since married Mehta, wants "Only that you should stick to the facts" (173), something Angelis's film—any work of art—cannot do completely.[4]

Hare's manipulation of art and reality demonstrates how ironically they coexist. At the end of the play, as the audience sympathies toward Stephen have reached their apex, those very feelings are undercut by the actor playing Stephen. Stepping out of Stephen's character, the actor offers Mehta a ride in his vintage car—a 1954 Alvis convertible—which he describes to Mehta as "my whole life" (229). In the midst of characters who might have been moved to rethink their own complacency as Mehta himself was, Stephen the actor emerges as an entirely unreflective, self-absorbed car collector. To him, nothing else matters.

Mehta himself, played by the same actor who plays him in the rehearsals, also disputes the way in which Stephen is portrayed: "Your film is a betrayal unless at the heart it is clear: for all the bitterness, for all the stupidity . . . you must see, we admired this young man" (222). Just as Stephen objected to the political opinions expressed in Mehta's novels, so Mehta now objects to the opinions expressed in the rehearsals as distinct from his own response to Stephen as an individual.

Sources   There is a curious coincidence in the appearance of Tom Stoppard's *The Real Thing* in London about nine weeks before *A Map of the World*. Both employ multiple, shifting perspectives through the use of plays-within-plays; both address the possibilities for political commentary within drama as well as the relationship between art and reality. But politically the two plays have nothing in common.

A Map of the World is for several reasons Hare's most Shavian work. Like Shaw's *Major Barbara*, Hare's play revolves around a bet between two men involved in an ideological contest for a woman. In Shaw, of course, what is at stake is the woman's soul; in Hare, the contest, first and foremost, is for her body and only unexpectedly for her soul as well. In *The Quintessence of Ibsenism*, Shaw describes the Discussion play, a new dramatic genre descended from plays like Ibsen's *A Doll's House*: "Formerly you had in what was called a well made play an exposition in the first act, a situation in the second, an unravelling in the third. Now you have exposition, situation, and discussion; and the discussion is the test of the playwright. . . . the serious playwright recognizes in the discussion not only the main test of his highest powers, but also the real centre of his play's interest."[5] In Hare's play, the discussion of world poverty is attenuated by Stephen's decision not to debate and then by his death. Yet the focus here is less on that issue than on, first, the relationship between art and reality and, second, the possibility for idealism. Those are the subjects that carry over from the Bombay story to the backstage story. Mehta never does renounce his political views but he very plainly recognizes the worth of his son's and Stephen's idealism.

Shaw's *The Quintessence of Ibsenism* also provides the categories for Hare's characters—Stephen the idealist, Mehta the realist, and Peggy the philistine—but in *A Map of the World* all three are converted, neither to the views of the realist nor to those of the idealist, but at least to admit the value of idealism.

Critical Reception *A Map of the World* first appeared at the Adelaide Theatre Festival in March 1982 and later transferred to the Sydney Opera House. The play's first London production opened at the National Theatre's Lyttelton Theatre on 27 January 1983. Although British newspapers make no secret of their political allegiances, there is little correlation between their politics and their critic's response to Hare's play. Conservative papers like the *Financial Times* and *Daily Telegraph* offered some of the play's most enthusiastic endorsements. On the other hand, Giles Gordon in the *Spectator* faulted Hare for not creating "flesh-and-blood individuals. His characters are embodiments of attitudes, credos, social posturing."[6] Similarly, Robert Cushman in the *Observer* wrote that the "characters have no existence outside their opinions."[7]

Although there was consensus that the acting, especially by Roshan Seth as Mehta, was admirable, the reviews were widely mixed. Negative reviews commented on the convoluted structure and ideological characters. John Russell Taylor in *Plays and Players* called the play "cockeyed" and wrote that Hare "has so built up Mehta's charms and plausibility that he seems to run away with the play."[8] Hare's longtime supporters took considerable pains to explain the play. Benedict Nightingale in the *New Statesman,* "the 'literary left-wing magazine' that presumably employs the play's protagonist," carefully outlined and convincingly refuted the various charges against *A Map of the World.* Nightingale concluded that the change in Mehta's character "is a synthesis, not a Pauline conversion," and praised the play as Hare's best to date.[9] Michael Coveney pointed out that "it is a sure sign of the play's richness and assurance that the separate worlds of interpretation and real argument are so distinctly laid out and yet so obviously confused."[10] And Michael Billington in the *Guardian* identified Hare's play as "an immensely artful construct . . . a Wildean work about world politics."[11]

Saigon: Year of the Cat

The Eastern setting of *Saigon: Year of the Cat* allies it with *Map of the World* as do its treatment of postcolonialism and its linkage of the political and the personal. *Saigon* grew directly out of a visit Hare made to Vietnam and a fellowship from the U.S./U.K. Bicentennial Commission that enabled him to spend most of 1978 in California. Like *Map of the World* and *Wrecked Eggs, Saigon* deals with Americans as national types as clearly discerned as Hare's British types. In *Saigon* both principal characters, an American and a Briton, are very much the product of their homelands. Each draws identity from a native country, yet each is estranged from it.

Barbara Dean, a fifty-year-old Englishwoman living in Saigon, works in a bank. Around her are the signs of imminent collapse as the American presence in Vietnam nears its end. When she interviews a Vietnamese applying for a loan, she explains that money is lent for no more time than the American presence in Vietnam is expected to last— a single year. Barbara inhabits a world of faded colonial splendor. The bank in which she works is an "old-fashioned commercial bank. Busy. Vaulted ceilings. Grandeur. Fans."[12] By night she visits the Cercle Sportif, a vestige of the French colonial presence now occupied mainly by Americans, including a Colonel Judd with whom she plays bridge. Judd introduces her to Bob Chesneau, twenty-eight, and a minor official at the American embassy. In fact, Chesneau's standard-issue car gives him away as a CIA agent, a "spook" (92). Barbara asks Chesneau for a ride home and then invites him in for a beer.

At the bank, where her countrymen Henderson and Haliwell devote most of their energies to following British soccer teams, the growing desperation of the Vietnamese becomes clear. The signs of panic have already begun to appear: a teller decides to leave the country; a customer brandishes a gun and demands to withdraw a large amount of cash.

Chesneau returns to Barbara wondering if, despite his being "very emotionally stupid" (97), he has correctly read her character. Their affair, which in all likelihood will last no longer than the American presence, begins as the collapse of the South Vietnamese government is already under way.

In his intelligence work at the embassy Chesneau interrogates captured enemy agents and often involves them in a confidence game. He can get more out of an agent by eliciting some trust from him than by abusing him. But once the agent talks he is disposable; indeed, he might well be thrown out of a helicopter. Although Chesneau retains some measure of innocence and goodwill about his work, that tactic becomes sadly emblematic of the Americans' relations with the Vietnamese. At a Christmas party given by an American official, Jack Ockham, Barbara argues that the Americans ought to formulate evacuation plans. Despite the career risks involved, Chesneau decides to speak up at the embassy.

Asking Barbara's advice about whether he should accept a position in Hong Kong, Henderson tells Barbara that he is in love with her. He seeks Barbara's approval for his career move since it will cost him any relationship he might have shared with her, but none is forthcoming.

As 1975 begins, American analysts anticipate another New Year's offensive from the North. By March the situation has deteriorated to the point that only one-quarter of South Vietnam and three coastal areas are still under South Vietnamese/American control. Ockham and other officials outline a strategy, formulated only within the last week, that will support the official line: "No panic" (111). Chesneau's best contact, Nhieu, tells him that the North Vietnamese intend to fight all the way to Saigon. Because of the defeat of the faction that favored negotiations with the South and the Americans, Nhieu now insists on obtaining his own exit visas. While Chesneau formulates a list of the two hundred most important local contacts, Ockham and the others barely tolerate Chesneau's concern with evacuation. Challenging the validity of Nhieu's information, the American ambassador sees Chesneau's evacuation plans only as preparations for defeat. What is needed, the ambassador repeatedly insists, is additional money from Washington. Having lost a son in the war, the ambassador refuses to admit that defeat is even a possibility.

When Chesneau visits Barbara one night after curfew, drunk, to apologize for his considerable absence, she tells him that from the outset of their affair she understood that he would have no commitment to her. She asks that he not treat her like a wife, tells him of the desperation among the Vietnamese, and chides him because the Americans are "inventing a fresh set of lies" (121). Echoing his embassy superiors, Chesneau says that they cannot know with certainty that the war is lost, to which Barbara counters: "In that case you're the only people who don't" (122).

When an enemy pilot penetrates the supposed security of defense lines to bomb the heart of Saigon, Chesneau asks, "When is that mad bastard [the ambassador] in that office going to realize we need to get out?" (123). Ockham reminds him that he is free to resign; Judd tells Chesneau his noisy insistence on evacuation is not only ineffective, but "self-indulgent" (124). Chesneau does what good he can by arranging a passport and ticket for Lhan, a woman who works at Barbara's bank. But not until Chesneau escorts South Vietnamese President Thieu to the airport do the evacuation efforts receive official sanction. Processing centers, complete with kitchens, are set up, but too little time remains.

In the final days before the fall of Saigon, droves of foreign officials leave the country without notice. Haliwell leaves the bank for lunch one day and does not return. Having captured the airport, the North has given the Americans twenty-four hours to complete their with-drawal; anyone who gets out now will have to go by helicopter. Only after a Vietnamese at the bank finally persuades Barbara that she, too, must leave does she go to the embassy to see Chesneau.

Approaching the embassy while "White Christmas," the signal for the American evacuation, plays on the radio, Barbara spots Haliwell in the crowd. Rescued, he says "for a moment you felt what it's like to be them" (142). As the helicopter carrying Barbara and Haliwell lifts off the embassy roof, Hare describes her as looking like "an old English spinster" (144). Not only has she left behind a promising relationship, but Barbara has no place to go.

Inside the compound, the frantic mood of the American staff is tinged with relief and humor. While the Vietnamese struggle desper-ately to reach the embassy, the American staff are confident that they will get out. Examining lists of agents and supporters, Chesneau won-ders how few of them will escape. Repeatedly Ockham and Judd, continuing the no-panic policy, urge restraint and calm. When Brad, an official at an American company in Saigon, contacts the embassy about the evacuation of his company's employees and their families, Judd reassures him just before the phone line is cut and with it any possibility of rescue. Steadily the anxiety and chaos increase as the moment of the evacuation's end approaches. On the final flight, Chesneau realizes how disastrous the evacuation has been: Brad, his employees, and families at Forbes Chemical will soon fall into the hands of the Viet Cong; the lists and identification cards of American supporters sit neatly on Chesneau's embassy desk. A less successful evacuation is difficult to imagine.

Characters   Like the characters in *A Map of the World,* Chesneau
and Barbara inhabit an insular world of faded but still fashionable
colonial hotels and diplomatic enclaves. Unlike the other Europeans at
the bank, Barbara recognizes and responds to the plight of the Vietnamese. Her fellow employees, Haliwell and Henderson, are oblivious to
the events around them. Haliwell, for instance, offers a remarkably
myopic reading of the London *Times:* "Look at this. Strikes. Industrial
chaos. The whole country seems to be going to hell" (99). He refers, of
course, not to Vietnam, but to Britain. Henderson decides to leave
Vietnam because he is unlikely to be promoted at the Saigon branch
office. In leaving his only interest is in himself and the approval he
hopes to gain from Barbara.

Like Susan Traherne in *Plenty* and Jean in *Wetherby,* Barbara loathes the
repressiveness of Britain. Barbara sums up the British for Chesneau by
saying: "The people are—odd. They're cruel to each other. Mostly in
silent . . . unexpected ways. It's an emotional cruelty. You feel watched,
disapproved of all the time" (103–4). In voice-over, she describes herself
as secretive, a quality she traces to her first affair, carried out with a friend
of her father's.

The only character to recognize the beauty of Saigon, Barbara never
seems especially frightened or anxious about the fall of the city. She
calmly arranges for the passports and tickets of bank employees desperate to leave Saigon. Although she writes to her mother in England,
Barbara knows that there is nothing to which she can return. While the
Americans revel in the idea of going home and the Vietnamese who
manage to escape have the prospect of a new life before them, Barbara's
prospects for the future are dim, if not nonexistent. Chesneau, too,
realizes the dangers for those who supported the Americans after Saigon
falls. When he tries to convince his superiors of the importance of
evacuation, they insist on a military perspective that sees the situation
as unfavorable but salvageable.

The affair between Chesneau and Barbara is unlikely not only because
she is nearly twice his age, but because of the chaos that envelops them.
The difference in their ages makes it plain that this may be a last chance
for Barbara, just as it is a last chance for the Vietnamese who have
supported the Americans. Like the "thing" that Anna and Archie have in
Licking Hitler or Susan Traherne's affair with Lazar, the relationship
between Barbara and Chesneau is heightened by the stress of wartime.

Barbara brings out Chesneau's finest instincts. Like the effect that
Caroline has on William in *Dreams of Leaving,* Barbara inspires

Chesneau to do his best work, to live up to his fast fading ideals. Unable to convince his superiors to implement evacuation plans, he feels no small measure of guilt and begins to avoid Barbara. He is guilty in her eyes alone; within the embassy itself, he is seen as an idealistic if slightly daft crusader. As Saigon's fall grows increasingly obvious, Chesneau finds it more difficult to face her because she reminds him of what he knows he should do and should be. When, after a long absence, he finally does visit her, he must fortify himself with drink and excuses.

Like the Americans in Vietnam, Chesneau thinks he has made a commitment in his relationship with Barbara. But in both cases, the commitments cannot be fulfilled. The final line, spoken by an American helicopter pilot, "We're all going home" (151), is as painful as it is ironic for Chesneau. Like Barbara, he appreciates what has been abandoned. Hare never challenges Chesneau's good intentions. A man who originally joined the CIA to avoid the draft, Chesneau conscientiously reports to the ambassador that they are on the brink of disaster, but his effort, the entire American effort, is finally botched. Promises were made that will not be kept. Faithful support personnel and their families have been assembled at evacuation points, but they will be collected by the Viet Cong, not by the Americans.

Most of the minor characters are hardened into a dogmatic position that admits no possibilities other than the official line. Jack Ockham and Colonel Judd see the situation only in military and never in personal terms. They remain as unsympathetic as they are undeveloped. Only the ambassador, who lost a son in the war, has method in what seems to be his madness.

Themes and Images   Hare draws upon distinctly American images, sometimes bordering on the cliché, that contrast strongly with the Vietnamese setting: a baseball game is played every noon at the American embassy; Chesneau's Ford Pinto gives him away as a CIA operative; the signal for the final evacuation is the broadcast of Bing Crosby's "White Christmas" on the radio.

While *Wetherby* deals with repressiveness, which Hare associates with the British, *Saigon* focuses on waste, which he identifies with Americans. *Saigon* is suffused with images of waste and futility. The American ambassador complains bitterly when ashes from the incineration of documents drift into his swimming pool. Exterior scenes in Saigon are described as "wasteground" (112). But the images of waste and futility also apply to the love affair that, like those in *Teeth 'n' Smiles, Knuckle,* and *Dreams of Leaving,* is destroyed. Late in the play, Barbara tells Chesneau her deepest regret: "It's the waste. All the time we've wasted" (139). In the larger political context, the image of waste epitomizes the American involvement in Vietnam—the waste of money, of energies, and of lives.

Visually *Saigon* counterpoints images of ordered opulence with those of chaotic desperation. In order to clear a landing area for the evacuation helicopter, the ambassador's favorite tree is chainsawed as he looks on in disapproval. "Dodge City," the processing center for evacuees, includes a complete kitchen to serve food. As the Communist forces ring the city, the French sit poolside at the Cercle Sportif. The ambassador's emergency fund—$2 million in cash—is ordered burned, then is stolen, and finally dropped from a helicopter onto the crowd trying to reach the embassy. The chaos of the final evacuation combines the atmosphere of a grotesque life-or-death game show and the spectacle of Grand Guignol. Absurdities and ironies abound: the only girl employed by the British Council at the library does not speak English; Vietnamese fighting to reach the embassy could not care less about the $2 million that rain down upon them; even after the phone lines are severed, Judd says "Nobody is going to get left behind" (147).

Hare's emphasis falls squarely on the personal rather than the political, the intimate rather than the historical. Like his best works, *Saigon* successfully counterpoints a personal relationship and background of political turmoil. Robert Chesneau and Barbara Dean are seen in a double perspective: for *what* they are—an American CIA operative and a British bank employee—and, more important, for *who* they are—individuals and lovers.

Broadcast and Critical Reception   *Saigon: Year of the Cat,* Hare's third published play for television, was directed by Stephen Frears, who has since directed Hanif Kureishi's *My Beautiful Laundrette* and *Sammy and Rosie Get Laid.* It was broadcast in November 1983 by Thames Television in Britain, and in April 1984 in Canada and the United States.

Much of the subtlety of *Saigon* succumbs to Frears's heavy-handed direction of the television play. Let two examples suffice: Chesneau often carries not only a handgun in a shoulder holster but another in his belt; at one point, wearing both of these guns, he also wields an automatic submachine gun. To bear out the stereotypical image of the spook, Jack

Oakham and the other CIA operatives not only wear sunglasses, but they wear them indoors—and indoors at night. Under Frears's direction, *Saigon* begins as a campy send-up of romance-during-wartime B-movies (like *Casablanca*) and quickly drifts into hyperbole. The casting of Frederic Forsyth and Judi Dench minimizes the age difference between Chesneau and Barbara as well as the youth and naïveté of a character who joined the CIA to avoid the draft.

Maclean's, a Canadian publication, identified "Hare's sometimes blatant anti-Americanism" as the film's single flaw. "Hare seems to presume that he understands Americans because he speaks the same language. His American characters . . . turn out to be stereotypes."[13] While it is true that Hare relies upon clichés like the embassy's daily baseball game to characterize the American presence, much of the complexity and sympathetic qualities of Chesneau are lost in the televised film.

The Bay at Nice

In Leningrad in 1956 Valentina Nrovka is asked to judge a work of art, her daughter, and herself. All three are tasks of "authentication." She is literally asked to authenticate a painting willed to the Soviet government by an expatriate aristocrat. Her daughter, Sophia, also wants authentication, in the form of her mother's approval of her intended divorce and remarriage. In evaluating the painting and her daughter, Valentina examines her own life and passes judgment on herself.

Museum authorities seek out Valentina because some forty years earlier she had studied under Matisse in Paris. Scientists have attempted to establish the authenticity of the work through a battery of empirical tests, but only Valentina can identify Matisse's unique "handwriting," the distinctive style that expresses its creator's spirit.

Valentina has no trouble understanding why an expatriate aristocrat willed this legacy to a Communist government; she made a similar decision in returning to the Soviet Union with her daughter in 1921. That choice cost Valentina her livelihood, her art, and her freedom. In Paris Valentina lived a bohemian life devoted to art, men, and pleasure. Returning to Russia with her daughter meant sacrificing her personal and her artistic freedom. Because her work does not conform to the dictates of Soviet socialist realism, Valentina has not exhibited her paintings for seventeen years. Like the count who bequeaths a valuable painting to his homeland, Valentina felt a profound attachment to her native country. Her love for her country and her daughter, a Russian child in Paris, lured her away from freedom. Moreover, she believed that choosing exile was cowardly.[14]

Her daughter, Sophia, now thirty-six years old, is a teacher, the mother of eight-year-old twins, and the wife of a party member. Weary of her responsibilities to the state and her family, Sophia wants to divorce her husband and marry Peter. Valentina stresses the wholly negative consequences of Sophia's divorce: the twins will likely despise their mother; everyone will suffer economically and emotionally; Sophia's first husband's career will probably founder; Valentina will have to sell her apartment to pay for the divorce. Moreover, Valentina describes Peter, a sanitation worker in his mid-sixties, as "the Soul of No Hope" (43). Despite all this, Valentina agrees to help her daughter; she will even try to convince Sophia's present husband not to oppose the divorce.

Characters   Valentina's practical, unsentimental approach to her daughter's request belies her principal motivation: love. Unlike Matisse, who had no time for love (32) because his energies were consumed by his art, Valentina says that "[l]ove was all I had time for. At least until the twenties" (33)—until, that is, she assumed her responsibilities. By returning to Russia with her child as well as by supporting Sophia's divorce, Valentina indicates her willingness to make sacrifices motivated by love. As she did thirty-six years ago, Valentina makes a choice that is neither self-interested nor self-serving.

Unlike many of Hare's heroines, Valentina recognizes and accepts the consequences of her decisions. She believes in discipline: the discipline in painting she learned from Matisse and the discipline of her own life learned from the consequences of her return to the Soviet Union. As she tells her daughter: "People should stick. They should stick with what they have. With what they know. That's character" (27). But underpinning Valentina's resolve is her profound sense of the loss of her freedom and her art.

With a reputation as a witch, she clearly intimidates practically everyone by being very outspoken—she calls Peter a silly, bald old man and terrifies the museum's assistant curator. She does not suffer fools gladly, but bears her losses stoically. Sophia describes her mother as characterized by an intolerance that stops just short of self-righteousness. Valentina's principles have cost her dearly; she defends those convictions with contempt for others.

Sophia is remarkable only for her self-centeredness. In contrast to her mother, Sophia wants to assert her freedom and cast off her commitments. From the little that Peter says, Sophia's attraction to him seems based on his grateful, emotional response to her.

Wrecked Eggs

At their country house in upstate New York, Loelia and Robbie, a couple in their late thirties, entertain Grace. Loelia and Robbie have invited lots of old friends, but Grace is the only person who attends a party planned as a rite of passage to celebrate their divorce. A publicity agent who secures coverage in the social columns for the rich and ambitious of Manhattan, Grace explains that "reading about success is the new pornography" (58). Their conversation quickly turns from an anecdote about a bigamist who was run down by a laundry truck to Grace's most recent abortion—neither her first nor her second. Loelia, too, has had more than one abortion.

Because he works so hard, Robbie turns the conversation to tales of his industry and success. Loelia and he have a $100,000 a year "nut"— the amount they need to earn to maintain what they have already acquired: a house on the Hudson river, a swimming pool, and all the attendant luxuries. Money, Robbie tells Grace, is a wonderful thing because "it puts a value on things" (67). To him money justifies or rewards whatever unpleasantness is involved in earning it.

An unlikely candidate to sanction the divorce of Loelia and Robbie, Grace met Loelia only a week earlier at a tennis lesson; she is now meeting Robbie for the first time. Initially Grace is embarrassed by their divorce announcement, but just as Loelia and Robbie want Grace's presence to commemorate their divorce, Grace wants something from Robbie and Loelia: some validation—an authentication, to use the language of The Bay at Nice—of her abortion: "I haven't got over it. That's why . . . I accepted to come. It was selfish. I needed to get away for this weekend" (68). Grace is entirely unwilling to make a commitment; specifically, she refuses to have a child. She asks her hosts rhetorically, "Do I really want a relationship that, in some form or other, will now have to last for the rest of my life?" (69)

As it turns out, it is Loelia's desire that she and Robbie should divorce. She agreed to stay for Robbie's party only on the condition that the divorce itself would not be discussed. Robbie and Loelia reminisce about their courtship. Loelia, a hippie at the time, wrote Robbie's father concerning his trial for treason and espionage. Loelia explains to Grace that Robbie's father was the celebrated spy William Dvořák who revealed the "operational details of nuclear submarines" (86). Robbie says he dislikes his father—his father's superiority, his claim that he understood "the need to defuse the cold war better than anyone" (87). In truth, Robbie despises his father, not for what he did to his country, but for what he did to him. Although Robbie purports to love America because of the "right to start again" (87) that it offers, his father apparently does not share that right.

Grace insists on how odd she finds the arrangements that others just take for granted—the butcher paying off protection money to some gangster; the ease with which Robbie and Loelia are splitting up. In the end, Loelia decides to accept Grace's advice that there are some standards in the world and to stay with Robbie—tentatively, for only a day longer.

Characters   As in earlier works, individuals are closely associated with a national identity. Robbie relates stories about a Japanese ship's captain who killed himself because he felt disgraced after his cargo fell into the sea and about funeral pyres in India. As Americans, what he, Grace, and Loelia sadly miss are the traditions and rituals attached to the important moments of life in contemporary America. "Celebrating" a divorce is as unlikely as commemorating an abortion—but these are the events that mark their lives and the lives of many modern Americans.

The Americans here are callow caricatures of rootlessness and ambition. Robbie, a workaholic lawyer, is a model of self-reliance and a near parody of the American work ethic. For him, material wealth is the only proof of the value of an individual. Judging a job purely on the basis of how much money it produces, he tells Grace: "If you make money, your job is a success . . . money is *straight*" (67)—"manly," objective, purely quantitative.

After first earning the audience's dislike for his maniacal devotion to material success and a grotesque American dream, Robbie emerges as a more sympathetic character because of his extreme vulnerability. Loelia, who repeatedly refers to Robbie as boyish, tells Grace that much of Robbie's behavior can be explained as a reaction against his father. In response to his father's "treason," Robbie became the incarnation if not the parody of all things American. Compulsive, hard-working, self-reliant, candid, rootless, stoic—he is a compendium of American qualities.

Robbie is thoroughly ambivalent about the past. On the one hand, he wants to "Cross out the past" (87); his ability to do just that is what he loves most about America. He has crossed out his disappointingly bookish son. He is about to cross out Loelia by divorcing her. He has long since crossed out his father. Yet, on the other hand, Robbie yearns for some tradition, some rootedness that will give his life direction and possibly allow him to discover or to create a true identity for himself. Lovingly, meticulously, he recalls his first meeting with Loelia, but he later says that he would like to forget the past, or at least to edit his father out of his memories. As it stands, he is virtually anonymous—defined only by his money and possessions, about to lose his connection with his wife (his present) as surely as he has severed the ties to his father (his past) and, most likely, his son (his future).

There is also a keen sense that as these characters face middle age they must find some identity for themselves, some way of dealing with disappointment. Loelia tells Grace, "Shit, I was born in Milton, Nebraska. They told me I'd be happy. I think I've got a right to do something else"—that is, to divorce Robbie even though he needs her (92).

Setting and Imagery   Images of excess abound. Loelia's many lovers, Grace's and Loelia's multiple abortions, the material comfort, and the lavish and exotic food all establish a sense of surfeit. Instead of the deprivation expressed in *The Bay at Nice, Wrecked Eggs* presents a vision of America as a land of grotesque plenty. Both Robbie and Loelia prepare separate meals, with enough food to feed dozens of people. Loelia's lines "There's food. You can have anything" (89) directly echo Susan Traherne's "There's plenty. Shall we eat again?" (58). And, as in *Plenty,* material indulgence not only corrupts, but engenders emotional and spiritual deprivation.

Beneath the prosperity and wealth in Rhinebeck, New York and in Manhattan is a persistent desperation and corruption that Hare earlier, especially in *Brassneck,* explicitly associates with capitalism. Grace, for example, tells of a project to wipe away the parks, old buildings, everything that "we call *life*" (76) on the west side of Manhattan to erect a huge, impersonal development: "It's dark, it's brutal, it's brown. It's eighty storeys of air-conditioned nothing. For no conceivable human purpose at all" (76). The title of the play, which refers to abortion, is yet another image of the waste and futility that Hare associates with Americans here, in *A Map of the World,* and in *Saigon.* As in the final scenes of *Saigon,* an incredible sense of waste characterizes *Wrecked Eggs.*

Hare's Americans are people who are primarily concerned with what people are like, not with what is right or wrong. Grace's job as a publicity agent is to present a public image of her clients as interesting or appealing so that their celebrity will mask their vacuity, greed, and corruption. In a curious echo of Willy Loman's conviction that success depends upon being "well-liked," Robbie argues that the person is more important to Americans than his or her deeds. If a jury likes a defendant, they are likely to find him innocent (58).

Common Themes   *The Bay at Nice* deals less with national types, certainly less with caricatures, than *Wrecked Eggs.* The immediate situation that links the plays on this double bill is that a woman is asked to sanction a marital break-up. More important, both deal with themes that Hare also addresses elsewhere: responsibility and commitment.

In many ways the plays are a study in contrast: whereas Valentina sacrifices her freedoms and accepts responsibilities, Robbie accepts only the responsibility to succeed financially and materially. In itself that is his way of rejecting his father. In fatherhood, marriage, and even friendship he is unable to sustain a relationship. The only person who shows up to celebrate his rites of divorce is a casual acquaintance of his wife's.

Grace describes herself in this way: "I've spent my life walking away from things. Which I can see is a luxury" (66). She refuses to have a child because it involves making a lifetime commitment, precisely the commitment that shapes Valentina's life. Yet, like Robbie, Grace laments the lack of standards and solidity in her life. Valentina, on the other hand, has spent the past thirty years of her life refusing to walk away from her native country, her daughter's selfish requests, and her own convictions. While Grace urges Loelia to make the kind of commitment she refuses, Valentina finds herself bound by the commitment she has made.

As different as America and Soviet society are, they both exert considerable pressure to conform on their inhabitants. But whatever commitments exist must come from personal choices. Loelia admires Robbie's father, still visits him in fact, because he had the courage to pursue his convictions. She wants to divorce Robbie because, as she tells Grace, "I'm trapped. With a man whose whole life is an attempt to pretend to be someone else" (90).

Critical Reception   Performed as a double bill in the Cottesloe Theatre, these two one-act plays were directed by Hare. Critics were virtually unanimous in praising Irene Worth's performance as Valentina and Zoe Wanamaker's performances as Sophia in *The Bay at Nice* and Grace in *Wrecked Eggs*. The praise the plays received as thought provoking and intelligent was often qualified by describing them as long-winded and moralizing. In general, most critics recognized that *The Bay at Nice* was vastly superior in characterization and subtlety to the relatively heavy-handed *Wrecked Eggs*. Michael Billington observed "that the American success-ethic . . . is as much a crippling ideology as communism; and that hacking out a personal morality is as difficult in a society of quickie divorce as in the puritanical Soviet Union."[15]

Chapter Nine
The Secret Rapture

The title of Hare's first full-length play since 1983, *The Secret Rapture,* refers to a nun's final union with Christ in death. For the protagonist of this play, Isobel Glass, death is the only escape from a world too brutal to tolerate her goodness. Hare himself describes *The Secret Rapture* as a play that deals directly with the question of good and evil, a theme that appears more clearly here than in any of his works since *Knuckle.* Isobel's secret rapture is the ultimate dream of leaving.

The play begins just after the death of Robert, father of Marion and Isobel and husband of Katherine. An idealist and pacifist, Robert owned a book shop in a small Gloucestershire village. Marion bursts into his room where his body still lies on the bed, hoping that she has not arrived too late—too late, that is, to reclaim an expensive ring she had bought her father as an "adequate"[1] expression of her love. In her father's bedroom she unexpectedly discovers her younger sister, Isobel, seeking a respite from the noise and confusion of the house.

Isobel, Marion, and Marion's husband, Tom, must deal not only with their grief but with Robert's widow, Katherine, an alcoholic of their own age. Marion, a junior minister for the Conservative government, sees Katherine merely as a problem to be solved. When Katherine proposes to move to London to work in Isobel's small design firm, Isobel initially refuses but, under pressure from Marion, she agrees to hire Katherine.

Isobel's design firm succeeds largely because of the pride and satisfaction that she and her two co-workers derive from their work. Within three weeks of joining the firm, Katherine drives out Isobel's and Irwin's only coworker, and the pride that Isobel and Irwin take from their work, like their relationship, begins to deteriorate. From the outset, their work provides at least Irwin with a real feeling of worth, one closely tied to his love for Isobel. Echoing William in *Dreams of Leaving,* Irwin tells Isobel: "I draw for you. That's what I draw. To please you. To earn your good opinion. Which to me means everything" (51). Irwin warns Isobel that she is being manipulated by her sister and stepmother, first by telling her, "Your father's dead. There is no family" (31), and later by reminding her, "There's such a thing as evil. You're dealing with evil" (58).

To accommodate Katherine's presence, Isobel and Irwin agree to accept a substantial investment—a takeover, in fact—offered by Tom's company. As chairman of a group calling itself Christians in Business, Tom sees no reason for Isobel not to trust him and to surrender control of her firm. Although reassured by both Tom and Marion, Isobel and Irwin are soon reduced to the status of mere members of a board of directors. No longer will they officially own or operate their business.

At the beginning of act 2, having missed the plane to a business meeting in Glasgow, Isobel returns to her posh new offices to find Irwin with Marion's assistant, Rhonda, who is lounging in a silk dressing robe while drinking champagne. Isobel missed her plane because Katherine attacked a client and was taken off to a psychiatric hospital. Isobel tries to break with Irwin, but to forestall a confrontation with him she agrees to go to a violent action movie with him and Rhonda. Disgusted, she walks out during the film, goes to Heathrow, and gets on the first plane which happens to be going to the Canary Islands, to escape the insistent demands of family, lover, and business. To Tom and Marion, Isobel's flight only confirms their perception of her irresponsibility and childishness. Isobel returns from her respite armed with her own convictions: to break with Irwin and with the business; to live in her father's house and prevent its sale; and to look after Katherine as best she can. Moreover, she returns changed—less willing than ever to argue, thinner, more haggard, but also calmer because these choices are her own. When Tom and Marion confront her with their plans to sell the business, she accepts their decision, acquiesces to their demands, and makes her own peace.

After weeks of separation from Isobel, Irwin grows miserable and angry. By the time he arrives at Katherine's apartment in the penultimate scene, he blames Isobel for his unhappiness: "It's you. You've destroyed me. I don't sleep. I can't make sense of life. . . . I feel worthless" (77). Katherine, who never had any moral sense to begin with, unlocks the door for Irwin, fails to recognize the danger he poses, and refuses to call the police. Isobel tells Irwin that he cannot force her to love him: "You can shoot me and hold my heart in your hand. You still won't have what you want. The bit that you want I'm not giving you. You can make me say or do anything you like. Sure, I'll do it. Sure, I'll say it. But you'll never have the bit that you need. It isn't yours" (77). When Isobel finally attempts to leave, he shoots her in the back.

In the last scene, Marion and Tom return to Robert's home where they now reveal some glimmer of insight into their own self-deception and unhappiness. For Tom, that recognition, faint as it indeed is, lies in his admission that lately he has "slightly lost touch with the Lord Jesus" (83)—his God of commerce and coincidence. Looking at his father-in-law's now deserted living room, Tom calls it a "perfect imitation of life" (83) whereas it was once, when Robert and Isobel were alive, life itself. And Marion senses that her lifelong anger is linked to her keenest childhood memory "of watching and always pretending" (82). While that does help to explain her ruthless detachment from life, Marion's final line, the last of the play, once again levels the implication of irresponsibility and guilt at the sister she has helped to destroy: "Isobel, why don't you come home?" (83).

Characters

Marion and Katherine incarnate Hare's obsession "with the cost of telling yourself or not telling yourself the truth. Choices of honesty."[2] Even early works like *The Great Exhibition* and *Knuckle* explore the human cost of self-deception and its often attendant self-pity. Blinded by their solipsism, neither Katherine nor Marion can see how disastrously they affect Isobel.

Marion has always lived at one remove from life. She despises human emotions because they are sloppy and not easily quantified. In the midst of her quandary over Isobel's abrupt flight, Marion wonders if Isobel's problem isn't simply a question of bad diet. Considering the possibility of sending her sister to a psychiatrist, Marion likens the human soul to an automobile: "It's like fixing a car. If it breaks, just mend it" (63). Later, her profound hatred of life clearly emerges as she tells Isobel, "You spoil everything you touch. . . . God, how I hate all this human stuff. Wherever you go, you cause misery" (70).

Different as Marion and Katherine are in personality, they are alike in their anger. Marion's unremitting rage mystifies even her husband: "She's got everything she wants. Her party's in power. For ever. She's in office. She's an absolute cert for the Cabinet. I just don't see why she's angry all the time" (7). Marion herself delights in doing battle: "That's what's great. That's what's exciting. It's a new age. Fight to the death" (38). What Marion does not recognize is how completely this philosophy permeates her life. She views everyone, including her sister, as an opponent to be overcome and vanquished.

While Marion's anger springs from her contempt and power (the two seem identical), Katherine's emanates from her own mediocrity and alcoholism (74), and culminates in her trying to stab a potential client with a knife at dinner, an episode that lands her in a psychiatric hospital. Addicted to the intoxicants of power and alcohol, Marion and Katherine shut out the emotional realities of life—their own and others'.

While Marion accepts her anger as an integral component of her fast-track career and Katherine grapples with hers, anger consumes Irwin as though it were an infectious disease. Irwin presumes much in his relationship with Isobel: that he and Isobel are a team; that she will support or at least accede to his decisions; that she will continue to love him. In the first scene in which he appears, he presumes to speak for Isobel in firing Katherine (34). In the next scene Isobel becomes aware that he has struck a deal with Marion and Tom about the takeover of their design firm; here he retracts what he earlier told Isobel about the folly of mixing family and business after he realizes that his salary is about to double. In scene 5 Irwin appears positively jealous of the time that Isobel devotes to Katherine. After that confrontation Isobel refuses even to be in the same room with Irwin. So unbalanced is Irwin by Isobel's rejection of him that he blames her for all his unhappiness and claims her in the only way he can imagine: by killing her.

The erosion of Irwin's relationship with Isobel and his seduction by the values of Marion and Tom precipitate Isobel's murder. What comes between Isobel and Irwin is not only what Irwin takes for granted, but also the insistence of Marion and Tom that they overextend themselves—personally and professionally. In personal terms, Marion and Tom want them to marry—to solidify and to legalize their relationship. In professional terms, Marion and Tom want them to expand—to move upscale by selling out to Tom's parent corporation. Tom's proposal to take over the firm poses a formidable array of arguments to Isobel: Irwin's salary will double; room will be made for Katherine; God, says Tom, will be pleased; and money will be made. Compelling as these points are, Katherine's reasoning is the most succinct and shameless: "Given what's going on, it's just stupid not to go and grab some of the dough for yourself" (41). When combined with his disappointment over losing Isobel, anger finally drives Irwin to madness and murder. Without Isobel's approval he feels worthless. From the moment that she hears Irwin in Katherine's

all forms of the interpersonal beastliness with the dominant political ethic."[7]

The New York production of *The Secret Rapture* gives new meaning to the phrase "critical controversy." Joseph Papp, the American producer, originally planned to run *The Secret Rapture* for just over five weeks in the New York Shakespeare Festival. After the *New York Times* decided to review that production, rather than waiting for the Broadway opening, Papp condemned the newspaper's policy as "destructive to our theater and its objectives, and an invasion of my prerogatives as a producer"[8] and drastically attenuated the play's run in the festival. On Sunday 22 October 1989 the *New York Times* ran an enthusiastic feature by Benedict Nightingale (who wrote a very positive review of the London production in the *Guardian*) on the play, Hare, and Blair Brown (Hare's girlfriend for whom he wrote both *The Secret Rapture,* specifically the role of Isobel, and the film *Strapless*).[9]

After several weeks of previews on Broadway, *The Secret Rapture* opened on 26 October 1989 to widely mixed reviews. Mimi Kramer in *The New Yorker* called the play "smug and obvious."[10] On the other hand, James Leverett writing for the *Village Voice* offered almost unqualified praise for Hare's "provocative and complex" play: "moving between great poles like chaos and order, spirit and matter, Hare might occasionally lose his way, but can still offer sudden blazing insights."[11] In *Newsweek,* Jack Kroll, who had on 9 January 1989 raved about the London production,[12] called *The Secret Rapture* "the best play of the year and the most compelling British import in years."[13] But Frank Rich's largely negative review in the *New York Times* certainly, as far as Hare was concerned, precipitated the abrupt closing of the New York production. Rich's review faulted Hare's direction and concluded: "Mr. Hare embraces the human, messy though it may be. To do otherwise is to forestall rapture until death or settle for a soulless existence that one character calls 'a perfect imitation of life.' What I don't understand is how a dramatist so deep in human stuff could allow so pallid an imitation of life to represent his play on a Broadway stage."[14] Hare wrote Rich a widely circulated letter protesting Rich's injudicious use of his vast powers as the most important New York (and, hence, American) critic. Rich later wrote Hare back a less well-publicized letter. Headlining its lead story as "Ruffled Hare Airs Rich Bitch," the 15 November 1989 issue of *Variety* quoted Hare as saying "I think Rich is totally irresponsible in the use of his power."[15] On 28 November 1989 the *Village Voice* ran a three-page story on the imbroglio between Hare,

Rich, and Kroll, who, caught up in the fray, was suspended from reviewing for *Newsweek*.[16]

Summation

Written just before Margaret Thatcher's re-election to a third term as prime minister, *The Secret Rapture* depicts the prevailing zeitgeist of Britain in the late 1980s as, in the words of the movie *Wall Street*, "greed is good." In this quantified world, Isobel's kindness, honesty, and integrity are not assets, only liabilities.

Isobel is a heroine of considerable strength and selflessness. Untinged by the ambiguity central to Susan Traherne and most of Hare's other heroines, Isobel very precisely recalls Jenny, whom Hare describes as "this girl who is meant to be a good person"[17] in *Knuckle*. Even in the face of adversity, hostility, ingratitude, and grief, Isobel maintains her idealism and values. She is undone not from within, but from without. Whereas drugs, alcohol, power, self-pity, despair, and madness destroy virtually all of Hare's previous heroines, what destroys Isobel is not a weakness of character. The worst that can be said of her is that she turns the other cheek. She is, in fact, virtually Christ-like in that the center of her life is love and compassion. In the original production, betrayed by Katherine and shot by Irwin, Isobel dies arms akimbo as if to confirm her secret rapture in death. But given the warped values that prevail, Isobel's death will change little in this rapacious world.

Conclusion

Commentators from fields as disparate as economics and film criticism often speak of a postwar British malaise. Labor historians see the labor unrest of the past forty years, with wildcat strikes, union upheavals, and worker demonstrations as its most telling symptoms. The religious historian traces the malaise to the secular if not godless rejection of traditional organized religion since World War II. Sociologists find in it the recalcitrant discrimination against people of color. Hare finds that malaise is the despair of promises unfulfilled, of hope squandered on false premises, of love eroded by society's pressures. Despite its political or social roots, the ultimate tragedy of Hare's characters is invariably personal, never simply abstract. His plays reflect the state of British society since World War II with an unremitting focus on the inextricable links between the private and the public, the personal and the political.

The dominant pattern to emerge from British drama and film since 1970 portrays conventional bourgeois life and its institutions as contemptible not simply because they are fraudulent or outmoded, but because they are soulless, loveless, vacuous, and debilitating. Inimical to life and especially to romance, contemporary society threatens to destroy whatever spirit its members retain.

History

Hare now says that he no longer considers himself a political playwright.[1] Certainly he is not one to use his works to advance a doctrinaire or dogmatic political agenda. At least since *Knuckle* he rejects works that "present ready-made solutions and set points of view."[2] In fact, he attributes much of the hostility his plays encounter to the fact that audiences and critics alike often balk at complicated situations and characters. As a writer he never advances a monolithic solution to his characters', let alone his audience's, problems. His plays are provocative, but hardly polemic.

Yet the context, the historical setting, of his most recent works is no less important than in his most political plays. From *Knuckle* to *The*

Secret Rapture Hare demonstrates that individuals cannot cut themselves off from the worlds they inhabit. Even Jean's Wetherby cottage and Robert and Isobel's Gloucestershire home, arcadian as they are, are not beyond the reach of society. In the plays that address global questions, responsibility is still most keenly felt on an individual level. That is the basis of Mehta's "conversion" from cynic to idealist in *A Map of the World*. Whether they recognize it or not, Hare's characters exist in systems that they shape—actively or passively—and that in turn shape them. To deny responsibility by cordoning off tidy areas of personal versus public affairs is to deceive oneself, to partake of the self-deception that characterizes Hare's villains. Whereas in *Fanshen* characters are coerced into political consciousness, in *The Secret Rapture* Tom and Katherine profess to be apolitical, although they must live with the consequences of a system they tacitly accept. And one consequence of that system is the disparagement of idealism. Responsibility and idealism always figure importantly in Hare's works, as does his implied or explicit attack on the capitalistic economy. In *A Map of the World* and *The Bay at Nice* questions of responsibility focus on the artist's challenge to show the inevitability of political consequences.

Both thematically, in *A Map of the World,* and structurally, as in *Wetherby,* Hare depicts the inextricable bonds between the personal and the political. Since *Teeth 'n' Smiles* Hare counterpoints the spiritual and emotional lives of his characters with historical events. Even *Wrecked Eggs,* among Hare's least political works, draws upon the political to inform the personal because Robbie's reaction to his father's treason is the determining episode in his life. Yet Hare never subordinates the psychological complexity and development of his characters to a didactic message. The personal side of his characters often reveals whatever political messages he offers. Hence, Hare is rarely doctrinaire in his politics. Despite Hare's objection, the label "political dramatist" is applicable, but it is so in the best sense of the term: not only does he bespeak a consistent and humane view of real social and political situations, but he is a talented and meticulous writer.

As he has matured as a dramatist, Hare has subdued the satirical topicality of his works to larger, more difficult questions. Tom, the Christian businessman in *The Secret Rapture,* not only elicits some of the hardiest laughs in the play, but then, as he realizes his responsibility for what happens to Irwin and Isobel, becomes much more human. Although the object of brilliant satire, Tom is hardly a cartoon.

Because the past takes on increasing importance for his characters, Hare has developed a variety of techniques to manipulate time. As the past informs the present, Hare dramatizes the passage of decades in the lives of many characters: sometimes—as in *Plenty* and *Wetherby*—to show a character's youth; other times—as in *Teeth 'n' Smiles* and *Licking Hitler*—to indicate what becomes of his characters. In his works for television and film, time is easily manipulated through flashforwards and flashbacks. As Jean attempts to rediscover her relationship with Jim some twenty years earlier in *Wetherby*, the linear progression of time is interrupted by flashbacks governed by her memory and imagination. Structurally, *A Map of the World* is Hare's most ambitious attempt to portray characters both before and after their transformation.

Contemporary British Landscape

Hare's depiction of Britain invariably carries class connotations. The stately country manor of Lord Minton in *Licking Hitler*, for instance, intensifies the isolation and vulnerability of Anna Seaton, as well as exacerbating Archie's resentment of her. Similarly, Brock's diplomatic postings outside of Britain, and the diplomatic enclaves in Saigon and Bombay, suggest the insular class privilege maintained in the colonial world. In *Plenty*, *Saigon*, and *A Map of the World* the postcolonial world figures importantly both as a setting for and as a cause of the characters' dislocation.

Hare's plays impart a strong sense of the enormous gap between common people and aristocrats, diplomats, and successful entrepreneurs. Often, as in plays that have as little in common as *Brassneck* and *The Secret Rapture*, the trappings of material prosperity spell doom to the romantic or spiritual lives of his characters. In *The Secret Rapture*, for instance, Marion and Tom provide Irwin and Isobel with handsome salaries and luxurious appointments that prove disastrous to their business and romantic relationship. Prosperity carries ominous connotations in Hare's work; its cost is usually emotional and spiritual bankruptcy—as demonstrated both in *Plenty* and *Wrecked Eggs*.

The brief glimpses of urban life in *Wetherby* are no less menacing than those of yuppie London. Jean's cottage is a retreat from the sterility of installations like the University of Essex, which are as cold and unyielding as the system they epitomize. The barren landscape that produces a gang of children smashing sticks in *Wetherby* also nurtures John Morgan.

Character Types

More than any male playwright since Tennessee Williams, Hare
portrays women convincingly. But unlike most male playwrights, Williams included, Hare avoids defining these women solely in relationship to men. The women in his works are best remembered not as
daughters, wives, and mothers, but as friends, lovers, and individuals.
Like the vast majority of women in Britain and America, all of them
work outside the home. They are artists, teachers, journalists, bankers,
politicians, designers, singers, television announcers, and farmers. No
other playwright portrays such an array of women from virtually every
class and occupation. Hare endows these women characters with perhaps more freedom than has any other playwright. Most often they are
unmarried, and if married, often unhappily so. Rarely do they have
children; in fact, abortions figure more prominently in his works than
do children. Almost all the women in his plays are involved in a
romance doomed by circumstances that owe much to political realities.
Probably the strongest, most striking similarity among his women
characters is their disillusionment—usually due to some promise about
the future that fails to materialize.

Typically Hare's characters must choose between capitulation or compromise on the one hand and insanity or anomie on the other. Many of
them, especially the women, end in madness or withdrawal. Vanessa,
the mother of three rapacious children in *Brassneck,* composes lunatic
poetry. In *Teeth 'n' Smiles* Maggie goes off to prison as a scapegoat for the
group's drug bust—a fate she not only accepts, but embraces. Susan
Traherne ends by peeling the wallpaper with her bare hands in a crazed
desire to strip away the exterior trappings that overwhelm her life.
Anna Seaton in *Licking Hitler* rejects the brutality of the world by going
off to live with an unwed mother in Wales. Caroline in *Dreams of
Leaving* lands in a sanitarium. In *Saigon* a broken love affair exiles
Barbara Dean, presumably to her loveless native Britain; hers is a
dismal future made even bleaker by her age and insight. Like Maggie,
Barbara fully appreciates the exile that awaits her, its injustice, frigid-
ity, and randomness. Jean, in *Wetherby,* finds at least momentary comfort in Langdon and in sharing Stanley's toast "to all our escapes" (92).
Among them, only Isobel in *The Secret Rapture* ends in the finality of
death.

Despite the great diversity in age, class, profession, life-style, and
outlook among these women, most are all distinctly British, and all are

disillusioned. No matter what environment Hare depicts—the nether-world of rock 'n' roll, the dignified reserve of the diplomatic corps, or the European enclaves in the third world—the frustrations and disappointments of these women are the common bond among them. Together they form a composite portrait of the British malaise that borders on madness, despair, and self-destruction.

Hare's villains, on the other hand, often adjust readily to their loss of ideals through self-deception and compromise. Anticipating the futility of his action, Curly decides not to expose his father's corruption and loses Jenny, and without any expression of loss or remorse. The bitterness and hatred that defines Archie Maclean in *Licking Hitler* is impenetrable. William in *Dreams of Leaving* seems to embody Arthur's vision of a generation "rolling down the highway into middle age. Complacency. Prurience. Sadism. Despair" (*Teeth 'n' Smiles,* 88).

Promise and Disillusionment

The idealism of Hare's characters almost invariably owes to some promise—implicit or explicit—made in childhood. They face situations in which their youthful expectations simply cannot withstand ever-diminishing possibilities. Inculcated with the sense, if not the delusion, of the nobility of their nation, its past, and their values, his idealists struggle to reconcile belief and experience. Some are seduced by conformity and compromise (as in *Knuckle* and *Dreams of Leaving*); others are swept away in a larger historical action (as in *Saigon*); some are simply struck down (as in *Map* and *The Secret Rapture*); but most are lured by the possibility of escape—through drugs and alcohol, into the British countryside, by flying off to the Canary Islands, in insanity or self-deception. All have dreams of leaving.

Fixed in the historical context of the postcolonial decline of Britain, Hare's characters are often destroyed by their experience of anger, unfairness, and despair. Whether a member of Parliament, a gunrunner, or a journalist, these characters are painfully aware of their loss of ideals: Hammett in *The Great Exhibition* wonders what became of the idealism that inspired the Aldermaston marches; Curly speaks of his day as a time when "there are no excuses left" (*Knuckle,* 71); William comes to London filled with lofty journalistic ideals that begin to erode after the approval of his first article. And for the women in these plays the promises of youth are even more empty. Susan in *Plenty* recalls her belief at the end of World War II that "there will be days and days like this" (206); Maggie remembers a priest who told her "you will think and feel the finest things in the world" (72); Loelia in *Wrecked Eggs* reports that "they told me I'd be happy" (92).

Because of events, often political, in the loveless worlds his characters inhabit, romances in Hare's plays end disastrously. Arthur and Maggie, Chesneau and Barbara, Irwin and Isobel, Lazar and Susan, Archie and Anna, Curly and Jenny, William and Caroline—all these couples are involved in relationships where promise is surpassed only by disappointment.

Notes and References

Chapter One

1. "David Hare: From Portable Theatre to Joint Stock . . . via Shaftesbury Avenue," editorial interview with David Hare, *Theatre Quarterly* 5 (1975–76): 108. Reprinted in *New Theatre Voices of the Seventies: Sixteen Interviews from "Theatre Quarterly" 1970–80,* ed. Simon Trussler (London: Eyre Methuen, 1981), 110–20.

2. Ibid. In his diaries, Peter Hall reports a conversation in which Christopher Hampton told him that Hare was head boy at Lancing. See *Peter Hall's Diaries,* ed. John Goodwin (London: Hamish Hamilton, 1983), 291.

3. See Hare's memoir, "Cycles of Hope and Despair," *Weekend Guardian,* 3–4 June 1989, 1–5 and 7.

4. Ronald Hayman, "David Hare: Coming Out of a Different Trap," *Times* (London), 30 August 1975, 9.

5. Arthur Marwick, *British Society since 1945* (Hammondsworth: Penguin, 1982), 74.

6. Peter Calvocoressi, *The British Experience: 1945–75* (London: Bodley Head, 1978), 228.

7. "From Portable Theatre," 108.

8. Julian Petley, "The Upright Houses and the Romantic Englishwoman: A Guide to the Political Theatre of David Hare," *Monthly Film Bulletin* 52 (March 1985): 71.

9. "A Lecture," in *Licking Hitler* (London: Faber & Faber, 1978), 68.

10. Kenneth Tynan, *A View of the English Stage: 1944–1965* (London: Methuen, 1975), 148.

11. Terry Browne, *Playwrights' Theatre: The English Stage Company at the Royal Court* (London: Pitman, 1975), 6.

12. Ibid., 12.

13. John Russell Taylor, *The Second Wave: British Drama for the Seventies,* (New York: Hill & Wang, 1971).

14. Tom Stoppard, "Ambushes for the Audience: Towards a High Comedy of Ideas," *Theatre Quarterly* 4 (1974): 4.

15. John Colville, *The New Elizabethans: 1952–1977* (London: Collins, 1977), 269.

16. Ibid., 274.

17. John Peter, "Meet the Wild Bunch," *Sunday Times* (London), 11 July 1976, 31.

18. "From Portable Theatre," 109.

19. Ibid.

20. Peter Ansorge, *Disrupting the Spectacle: Five Years of Experimental and Fringe Theatre in Britain* (London: Pitman, 1975), 1.

21. Robert Hewison, *Too Much: Art and Society in the Sixties* (London: Methuen, 1986), 205.

22. Michael Codron produced *Slag, The Great Exhibition,* and *Knuckle* as well as the premieres of Pinter's *The Birthday Party* and *The Caretaker,* Stoppard's *The Real Inspector Hound,* and Hampton's *The Philanthropist.*

23. *Peter Hall's Diaries,* 92.

24. John Walker, "Top Playwrights," *Sunday Times Magazine* (London), 26 November 1978, 70.

25. Ansorge, *Disrupting the Spectacle,* 11.

26. Peter, "Wild Bunch," 31.

27. Catherine Itzin, *Stages in the Revolution: Political Theatre in Britain since 1968* (London: Methuen, 1980), 330.

28. W. Stephen Gilbert, review of *Plenty, Plays and Players,* June 1978, 29.

29. Simon Trussler, *New Theatre Voices of the Seventies* (London: Methuen, 1981), 110.

30. "From Portable Theatre," 111.

31. John Bull, *New British Political Dramatists: Howard Brenton, David Hare, Trevor Griffiths, and David Edgar* (London: Macmillan, 1984), 62.

32. Colin Chambers and Mike Prior, *Playwrights' Progress: Patterns of Postwar British Drama* (Oxford: Amber Lane Press, 1987), 187.

33. Pam Cook, review of *Plenty, Monthly Film Bulletin* 52 (November 1985): 345.

34. Michelene Wandor, *Look Back in Gender* (London: Methuen, 1987), 115.

35. Ronald Hayman, *British Theatre since 1955: A Reassessment* (London: Oxford University Press, 1979), 80.

36. Kenneth Tynan, *Show People* (New York: Simon & Schuster, 1979), 49.

37. Hayman, *British Theatre since 1955,* 82.

38. "From Portable Theatre," 113.

39. "A Lecture," 66.

40. Ibid., 61.

Chapter Two

1. Howard Brenton quoted in Peter Ansorge, "Underground Explorations: Portable Playwrights," *Plays and Players,* February 1972, 16.

2. *How Brophy Made Good,* in *Gambit* 17 (1971): 103; hereafter cited in the text.

3. For an account of the French situationists see Greil Marcus, *Lipstick*

Traces: A Secret History of the Twentieth Century (Cambridge: Harvard University Press, 1989).

4. *Slag* (London: Faber & Faber, 1971), 11; hereafter cited in the text.
5. "From Portable Theatre," 111.
6. Ruby Cohn, "Shakespeare Left," *Theatre Journal* 40 (1988): 49.
7. Ibid., 50
8. Ibid.
9. "From Portable Theatre," 110.
10. Clive Barnes, review of *Slag, New York Times,* 22 February 1971, 22.
11. "From Portable Theatre," 115.
12. *The Great Exhibition* (London: Faber & Faber, 1972), 26; hereafter cited in the text.
13. Ansorge, "Underground Explorations," *Plays and Players,* February 1972, 18.
14. Mary Holland, review of *The Great Exhibition, Plays and Players,* April 1972, 40.
15. Ansorge, "Underground Explorations," 18.
16. "From Portable Theatre," 113.

Chapter Three

1. "From Portable Theatre," 111.
2. Ibid., 110.
3. *Lay By,* in *Plays and Players,* November 1971, 69; hereafter cited in the text.
4. "From Portable Theatre," 112.
5. Ibid., 113.
6. Ansorge, "Current Concerns: Trevor Griffiths and David Hare Outline the Problems of Two Contemporary Playwrights," *Plays and Players,* July 1974, 18.
7. *Brassneck* (London: Methuen, 1974), 12; hereafter cited in the text.
8. Marion Johnson, *The Borgias* (New York: Holt, Rinehart, & Winston, 1981), 41.
9. Ibid., 196.
10. *Pravda* (London: Methuen, 1985), 124; hereafter cited in the text.
11. Playbill for *Pravda,* National Theatre, 1985.
12. "Joint Stock: A Memoir," *Granta* 18 (1986): 250.
13. "From Portable Theatre," 114.
14. William Gaskill, *A Sense of Direction: Life at the Royal Court* (London: Faber & Faber, 1988), 136.
15. *Fanshen,* in *The Asian Plays* (London: Faber & Faber, 1986), 5; hereafter cited in the text.
16. "A Lecture," 62.
17. Ibid., 64.

18. Ibid., 63.
19. "Joint Stock: A Memoir," 254.
20. Michael Coveney, review of *Fanshen*, *Plays and Players*, June 1975, 31.
21. Howard Brenton, "Petrol Bombs through the Proscenium Arch," *New Theatre Voices of the Seventies*, 91–92.

Chapter Four

1. "A Lecture," 64–65.
2. Ibid., 68.
3. David Geherin, *The American Private Eye* (New York: Ungar, 1985), 138.
4. *Knuckle*, in *The History Plays* (London: Faber & Faber, 1986), 26; hereafter cited in the text.
5. Harold Hobson, *Theatre in Britain: A Personal View* (Oxford: Phaidon, 1984), 220.
6. "From Portable Theatre," 113–14.
7. Jonathan Hammond, review of *Knuckle*, *Plays and Players*, April 1974, 40.
8. Michael Billington, review of *Knuckle*, in *Plays in Review 1956–1980: British Drama and the Critics*, ed. Gareth Evans and Barbara Lloyd Evans (New York: Methuen, 1985), 198.
9. *Teeth 'n' Smiles* (London: Faber & Faber, 1976), 16; hereafter cited in the text.
10. "A Lecture," 68.
11. Hare's frequent collaborator Nick Bicât composed the music for *Teeth 'n' Smiles;* Tony Bicât wrote the lyrics. Hare probably made at least some contribution because the lyrics to "Close to Me" include lines that appear to refer to the name of the club in *Knuckle:* "The shadow of the moon / In an age of miracles / As sharp as any knife."
12. Charles Lewsen, review of *Teeth 'n' Smiles*, *Times* (London), 3 September 1975, 10.
13. Ronald Bryden, review of *Teeth 'n' Smiles*, *Plays and Players*, November 1975, 22.
14. "A Lecture," 69.

Chapter Five

1. "Talk of the Town," *New Yorker*, 24 January 1983, 32.
2. "A Note on Performance," in *Plenty* (New York: New American Library, 1983), 88.
3. *Plenty*, in *The History Plays*, 140; hereafter cited in the text.
4. "A Note on Performance," 87.

5. Steve Lawson, "Hare Apparent," *Film Comment*, October 1985, 22.

6. See Mel Gussow, "A British Hedda?," *New York Times*, 20 April 1980, sec. 2, p. 3.

7. Bernard Levin, review of *Plenty*, *Sunday Times* (London), 16 April 1978, 37.

8. W. Stephen Gilbert, review of *Plenty*, *Plays and Players*, June 1978, 28.

9. Ibid., 29.

10. Irving Wardle, review of *Plenty*, *Times* (London), 13 April 1978, 7.

11. Frank Rich, review of *Plenty*, *New York Times*, 22 October 1982, C4.

12. Clive Barnes, review of *Plenty*, *New York Post*, 2 January 1983; reprinted in *New York Theatre Critics' Reviews*, January 1983, 397.

Chapter Six

1. *Scum* was commissioned by the BBC for the "Play for Today" series. After consultation with the Home Office, the television production was banned because "all the incidents portrayed could happen, but . . . they could not all happen in such a limited period of time." See "Play for Another Day," *Times Educational Supplement* (London), 27 January 1978, 2.

2. David Rose produced and Hare directed both *Licking Hitler* and *Dreams of Leaving* for BBC-1. Broadcast in January 1978 and January 1980, respectively, both are preserved in the BBC archives. *Saigon* was made for Thames Television and is available on videotape in Britain. Initially released as a commercial film, *Wetherby* was made in conjunction with Zenith Productions and Film Four International for Britain's Channel 4.

3. Petley, "Upright Houses and the Romantic Englishwoman," 72.

4. Introduction to *The History Plays*, 15.

5. *Licking Hitler*, in *The History Plays*, 95; hereafter cited in the text.

6. See Sefton Delmar, *Black Boomerang* (New York: Viking, 1962), 25.

7. Introduction to *The History Plays*, 13.

8. "A Lecture," 67.

9. *Dreams of Leaving* (London: Faber & Faber, 1980), 18; hereafter cited in the text.

Chapter Seven

1. *Wetherby* (London: Faber & Faber, 1985), 10; hereafter cited in the text.

2. Howard Brenton uses images of violence in the games of children to evoke a similar response in *Hitler Dances* (London: Methuen, 1982).

3. Mel Gussow, "David Hare: Playwright as Provocateur," *New York Times Magazine*, 29 September 1985, 45.

4. Richard Corliss, review of *Wetherby*, *Time*, 19 August 1985, 70.

5. Rex Reed, review of *Wetherby, New York Post,* 19 July 1985, 26.

6. David Sterritt, review of *Wetherby, Christian Science Monitor,* 19 July 1985, 23.

7. Andrew Sarris, review of *Wetherby, Village Voice,* 23 July 1985, 51.

8. Jill Forbes, review of *Wetherby, Sight and Sound* (Spring 1985): 140.

9. Lawson, "Hare Apparent," 22.

10. Quoted from the film *Plenty.*

Chapter Eight

1. *A Map of the World,* in *The Asian Plays,* 164; hereafter cited in the text.

2. Gussow, "Playwright as Provocateur," 47.

3. Benedict Nightingale, review of *A Map of the World,* in *London Theatre Record* 3 (1983): 48.

4. In the 1982 Faber & Faber edition of the play, Angelis appreciates Peggy's anxieties about the film's depiction of events from her life when he tells the cast: "For us it's a movie. For Peggy it is life" (28).

5. George Bernard Shaw, *The Quintessence of Ibsenism* (New York: Hill & Wang, 1957), 171.

6. Giles Gordon, review of *A Map of the World, London Theatre Record* 3 (1983): 48.

7. Robert Cushman, review of *A Map of the World, London Theatre Record* 3 (1983): 45.

8. John Russell Taylor, reivew of *A Map of the World, Plays and Players,* March 1983, 31.

9. Nightingale, review of *A Map of the World,* 48.

10. Michael Coveney, review of *A Map of the World, London Theatre Record* 3 (1983): 44.

11. Michael Billington, review of *A Map of the World, London Theatre Record* 3 (1983): 44.

12. *Saigon: Year of the Cat,* in *The Asian Plays,* 86; hereafter cited in the text.

13. John Bemrose, review of *Saigon, Maclean's,* 30 April 1984, 65.

14. *The Bay of Nice and Wrecked Eggs* (London: Faber & Faber, 1986), 39; hereafter cited in the text.

15. Michael Billington, review of *The Bay at Nice and Wrecked Eggs, London Theatre Record* 6 (1986): 972.

Chapter Nine

1. *The Secret Rapture* (London: Faber & Faber, 1988), 3; hereafter cited in the text.

2. Lawson, "Hare Apparent," 18.

3. Playbill for *King Lear,* National Theatre, 1986.

4. Michael Billington, review of *The Secret Rapture, Guardian Weekly,* 6 October 1988, 25.

5. Michael Coveney, review of *The Secret Rapture, Financial Times,* 7 October 1988, 17.

6. Michael Ratcliffe, review of *The Secret Rapture, Observer,* 9 October 1988, 43.

7. John Turner, review of *The Secret Rapture, Times Literary Supplement* (London), 14–20 October 1988, 1148.

8. Mervyn Rothstein, "Papp Hastens Uptown Move for Hare's 'Secret Rapture,' " *New York Times,* 29 August 1989, 15. The *New York Times* typically does review off-Broadway productions before they move to Broadway.

9. Benedict Nightingale, "David Hare Captures His Muse on Stage," *New York Times,* 22 October 1989, sec. H., pp. 5, 24–25.

10. Mimi Kramer, review of *The Secret Rapture, The New Yorker,* 13 November 1989, 113.

11. James Leverett, review of *The Secret Rapture, Village Voice,* 7 November 1989, 107.

12. Jack Kroll, "The Ladies of London," *Newsweek,* 9 January 1989, 52–53.

13. Jack Kroll, review of *The Secret Rapture, Newsweek,* 13 November 1989, 89.

14. Frank Rich, review of *The Secret Rapture, New York Times,* 27 October 1989, sec. C., p. 3.

15. Richard Hummler, "Ruffled Hare Airs Rich Bitch," *Variety,* 15 November 1989, 1.

16. Geoffrey Stokes, "The Secret Rupture," *Village Voice,* 28 November 1989, 37–39.

17. "From Portable Theatre," 112.

Chapter Ten

1. Vera Lustig, "Soul Searching," *Drama* 170 (1988): 18.

2. Tom Dewe Matthews, "Licking Thatcher," *Arena* 13 (1988–89): 159.

Selected Bibliography

PRIMARY WORKS

Collected Plays

The Asian Plays. London: Faber & Faber, 1986. *Fanshen, Saigon: Year of the Cat, A Map of the World,* and an introduction by the author.
The History Plays. London: Faber & Faber, 1986. *Knuckle, Licking Hitler, Plenty,* and an introduction by the author.

Individual Plays

"The Bay at Nice" and "Wrecked Eggs." London: Faber & Faber, 1986.
Dreams of Leaving. London: Faber & Faber, 1980.
Fanshen. London: Faber & Faber, 1976.
The Great Exhibition. London: Faber & Faber, 1972.
How Brophy Made Good. Gambit 17 (1971): 84–125.
Knuckle. London: Faber & Faber, 1973.
Licking Hitler: A Film for Television. London: Faber & Faber, 1978. Contains "A Lecture" delivered at King's College, Cambridge University, 5 March 1978.
A Map of the World. London: Faber & Faber, 1982.
Plenty. London: Faber & Faber, 1978. New York: New American Library, 1983 (contains "A Note on Performance" by Hare not found in the British edition).
Saigon: Year of the Cat. London: Faber & Faber, 1983.
The Secret Rapture. London: Faber & Faber, 1988.
Slag. London: Faber & Faber, 1971.
Teeth 'n' Smiles. London: Faber & Faber, 1976.
Wetherby. London: Faber & Faber, 1985.

Collaborations

With Howard Brenton. *Brassneck.* London: Methuen, 1974.
———. *Pravda: A Fleet Street Comedy.* London: Methuen, 1985.
With Howard Brenton, Brian Clark, Trevor Griffiths, Steven Poliakoff, Hugh Stoddart, and Snoo Wilson. *Lay By.* In *Plays and Players,* November 1971, 65–75.

Articles and Addresses

"Ah, Mischief: The Role of Public Broadcasting." In *Ah, Mischief: The Role of Public Broadcasting,* edited by Frank Pike, 41–50. London: Faber & Faber, 1982.
"Cycles of Hope and Despair." *Weekend Guardian,* 3–4 June 1989, 1–5 and 7.
"How to Spend a Million." *Sunday Times* (London), 3 March 1985, 39.
"Joint Stock: A Memoir." *Granta* 18 (1986): 247–54.
"A Lecture." In *Licking Hitler: A Film for Television.* London: Faber & Faber, 1978.

SECONDARY WORKS

Interviews and Interview Profiles

"After Fanshen: A Discussion." In *Performance and Politics in Popular Drama: Aspects of Popular Entertainment 1800–1976,* edited by David Bradby, Louis James, and Bernard Sharratt, 297–314. Cambridge: Cambridge University Press, 1980.
Ansorge, Peter. "Current Concerns: Trevor Griffiths and David Hare Outline the Problems of Two Contemporary Playwrights." *Plays and Players,* July 1974, 18–22.
———. "Underground Explorations: Portable Playwrights." *Plays and Players,* February 1972, 14–23.
Busby, Anne. "David Hare." National Theatre playbill for *The Secret Rapture,* 1988.
"David Hare: From Portable Theatre to Joint Stock . . . via Shaftesbury Avenue." *Theatre Quarterly* 5 (1975–76): 108–15. Reprinted in *New Theatre Voices of the Seventies: Sixteen Interviews from "Theatre Quarterly" 1970–80,* ed. Simon Trussler, 110–20. London: Eyre Methuen, 1981.
Ford, John. "Getting the Carp Out of the Mud." *Plays and Players,* November 1971, 20, 71.
Hayman, Ronald. "David Hare." *Times* (London), 22 May 1971, 19.
———. "David Hare: Coming Out of a Different Trap." *Times* (London), 30 August 1975, 9.
Hubert, Hugh. "Putting the Knuckle In." *Guardian,* 4 March 1974, 8.
Lawson, Steve. "Hare Apparent." *Film Comment,* October 1985, 18–22.
Lustig, Vera. "Soul Searching." *Drama* 170 (1988): 15–18.
Matthews, Tom Dewe. "Licking Thatcher." *Arena* 13 (1988–89): 159–60.
Nightingale, Benedict. "David Hare Captures His Muse on Stage." *New York Times,* 22 October 1989, sec. H, pp. 5, 24–25.

Petley, Julian. "The Upright Houses and the Romantic Englishwoman: A
Guide to the Political Theatre of David Hare." *Monthly Film Bulletin* 52
(March 1985): 71–72.
"Profile: David Hare, Playwright of Conviction." *Independent*, 8 October 1988,
14.
"Talk of the Town." *New Yorker*, 24 January 1983, 32.
Tynan, Kathleen. "Dramatically Speaking." *Interview*, February 1989, 80,
128–29.
Wilkes, Angela. "Making Fun of Fleet Street." *Times* (London), 16 December
1984, 37.

Bibliography

Page, Malcolm, and Ria Julian. "Theatre Checklist No. 8: David Hare."
Theatrefacts 8 (1976): 2–4, 10. Includes a brief chronology of Hare's life
and synopses of plays.

Books

Ansorge, Peter. *Disrupting the Spectacle: Five Years of Experimental and Fringe
Theatre in Britain.* London: Pitman, 1975. The first chapter, "Running
Wild," deals with the Portable playwrights: Hare, Brenton, and Wilson.
Booker, Christopher. *The Neophiliacs.* Boston: Gambit, 1970. An eccentric
but insightful social chronicle of Britain in the 1960s.
Brenton, Howard. *Hitler Dances.* London: Methuen, 1982.
Browne, Terry. *Playwrights' Theatre: The English Stage Company at the Royal
Court.* London: Pitman, 1975. Chronological account of the founding
and development of the Royal Court.
Bull, John. *New British Political Dramatists: Howard Brenton, David Hare,
Trevor Griffiths, and David Edgar.* London: Macmillan, 1984. Excellent
chapter on Hare.
Calvocoressi, Peter. *The British Experience: 1945–75.* London: Bodley Head,
1978. An informed, wide-ranging economic history of Britain in the
three decades after World War II.
Chambers, Colin, and Mike Prior. *Playwrights' Progress: Patterns of Postwar
British Drama.* Oxford: Amber Lane Press, 1987. Written before *The
Secret Rapture*, the chapter on Hare sees him as a playwright of the
seventies adrift in the eighties.
Childs, David. *Britain since 1945: A Political History.* London: Methuen,
1986. Covers domestic and foreign political issues through Thatcher's
second term.
Colville, John. *The New Elizabethans: 1952–1977.* London: Collins, 1977.
Convincing synthesis of social, political, and cultural trends covering
twenty-five years of British history.

Craig, Sandy, ed. *Dreams and Deconstructions: Alternative Theatre in Britain.* Ambergate: Amber Lane Press, 1980. Focuses on experimental and political theater since the 1960s.

Delmar, Sefton. *Black Boomerang.* New York: Viking, 1962. The autobiography of a black propagandist that supplies the model for events in *Licking Hitler.*

Evans, Gareth, and Barbara Lloyd Evans, eds. *Plays in Review 1956–1980: British Drama and the Critics.* New York: Methuen, 1985. An anthology of the initial reviews of important British productions from 1956 through 1980.

Gaskill, William. *A Sense of Direction: Life at the Royal Court.* London: Faber & Faber, 1988. The candid memoirs of the leading British director to espouse Brechtian techniques.

Geherin, David. *The American Private Eye.* New York: Ungar, 1985. Critical survey of detectives in American fiction.

Hall, Peter. *Peter Hall's Diaries.* Edited by John Goodwin. London: Hamish Hamilton, 1983. The voluminous account of Hall's theatrical activities between 1972 and 1980.

Hayman, Ronald. *British Theatre since 1955: A Reassessment.* London: Oxford University Press, 1979. Groups the works of Hare, John Arden, Edward Bond, and John McGrath under the rubric "the politics of hatred."

Hewison, Robert. *Too Much: Art and Society in the Sixties 1960–75.* London: Methuen, 1986. The third volume in Hewison's superb trilogy on the arts in Britain since 1939.

Hobson, Harold. *Theatre in Britain: A Personal View.* Oxford; Phaidon, 1984. Appreciation of the plays Hobson judges best and most influential since the 1960s.

Itzin, Catherine. *Stages in the Revolution: Political Theatre in Britain since 1968.* London: Methuen, 1980. A year-by-year chronicle of the companies and playwrights responsible for the politicization of British theater from 1968 to 1978.

Johnson, Marion. *The Borgias.* New York: Holt, Rinehart and Winston, 1981. A recent history of the Borgia family.

Marcus, Greil. *Lipstick Traces: A Secret History of the Twentieth Century.* Cambridge: Harvard University Press, 1989. Brilliant alternative history linking punk music and the French situationists.

Marwick, Arthur. *British Society since 1945.* Hammondsworth: Penguin, 1982. Social history of Britain that focuses on "that topic all-absorbing: class."

Ritchie, Rob. *The Joint Stock Book: The Making of a Theatre Collective.* London: Methuen, 1988. A chronology of productions by Joint Stock supplemented by essays and notes by Hare and others in the company.

Shaw, George Bernard. *The Quintessence of Ibsenism.* New York: Hill & Wang,

1957. The landmark analysis of Ibsen that includes Shaw's definition of a Discussion play and his description of characters as idealists, realists, and philistines.

Taylor, John Russell. *The Second Wave: British Drama for the Seventies.* New York: Hill & Wang, 1971. Brief sections on newcomers to British playwrighting.

Trussler, Simon, ed. *New Theatre Voices of the Seventies: Sixteen Interviews from "Theatre Quarterly" 1970–80.* London: Eyre Methuen, 1981. Important anthology of interviews with brief introductory comments.

Tynan, Kenneth. *A View of the English Stage: 1944–1965.* London: Methuen, 1975. A compilation of reviews and essays by the most influential critic and dramaturge since World War II.

————. *Show People.* New York: Simon & Schuster, 1979. Five profiles in entertainment, originally published in the *New Yorker,* including one on Tom Stoppard.

Wandor, Michelene. *Look Back in Gender.* London: Methuen, 1987. Feminist critique of postwar British drama, including brief analyses of *Slag* and *Teeth 'n' Smiles.*

Waugh, Evelyn. *A Little Learning.* Boston: Little, Brown, 1964. Autobiography that includes Waugh's recollection of his education at Lancing College.

Articles

Ansorge, Peter. Review of *Brassneck. Plays and Players,* November 1973, 63– 65. Enthusiastic response to the epic stagecraft and political metaphors in *Brassneck.*

————. "David Hare: A War on Two Fronts." *Plays and Players,* April 1978, 12–16. Excellent appreciation of Hare's plays up to and including *Plenty.*

Barlas, Chris. Review of *Lay By. Plays and Players,* November 1971, 47–48. Sees "familiar patterns" in the play's "insistence on the nastier side of life."

Barnes, Clive. Review of *Slag. New York Times,* 22 February 1971, 22. High praise for Hare's first American production.

————. Review of *Plenty. New York Post,* 2 January 1983. Reprinted in *New York Theatre Critics' Reviews,* January 1983, 397. Lauds *Plenty* as "a rich fantasy-tapestry . . . beautiful in its detailing."

Bemrose, John. Review of *Saigon: Year of the Cat. Maclean's,* 30 April 1984, 65. Canadian reviewer's favorable comments on the television production of *Saigon.*

Bigsby, C. W. E. "The Language of Crisis in British Theatre: The Drama of Cultural Pathology." In *Contemporary English Drama,* edited by C. W. E.

Bigsby. *Stratford-upon-Avon Studies:* 19 (1981): 11–51. Brief but excellent discussion of Hare's portrayal of England in despair.

Billington, Michael. Review of *The Bay at Nice and Wrecked Eggs, London Theatre Record* 6 (1986): 972. Very favorable review in the *Guardian.*

————. Review of *A Map of the World. London Theatre Record* 3 (1983): 44. Welcomes Hare's move to global affairs in "an immensely artful construct."

————. Review of *The Secret Rapture. Guardian Weekly,* 6 October 1988, 25. Positive reception of the London premiere of *The Secret Rapture.*

Bryden, Ronald. Review of *Teeth 'n' Smiles. Plays and Players,* November 1975, 21–2?. Mixed review that faults Hare's "over-willed, show off" tendencies.

Cohn, Ruby. "Shakespeare Left." *Theatre Journal* 40 (1988): 48–60. Shakespeare's modern offshoots in Hare's *Slag* and works by other contemporary playwrights.

Cook, Pam. Review of *Plenty. Monthly Film Bulletin* 52 (November 1985): 345. Generally unsympathetic review of the film version of *Plenty.*

Corliss, Richard. Review of *Wetherby. Time,* 19 August 1985, 70. Mixed review of *Wetherby.*

Coveney, Michael. Review of *Fanshen. Plays and Players,* June 1975, 31. Very favorable review that praises Hare's "beautifully written play."

————. "Beyond the Fringe." *Sunday Times Magazine* (London), 26 November 1978, 73. Overview of a decade of alternative theater in Britain.

————. Review of *A Map of the World. London Theatre Record* 3 (1983): 44. Largely positive reception of the first London production.

————. Review of *The Secret Rapture. Financial Times,* 7 October 1988, 17. Favorable review of the original London production.

————. "Turning Over a New Life." *Plays and Players,* June 1975, 10–13. Interview with the directors and actors of *Fanshen.*

Cushman, Robert. Review of *A Map of the World. London Theatre Record* 3 (1983): 45. Mediocre review that finds little substance in the play.

Edgar, David. "Ten Years of Political Theatre, 1968–78." *Theatre Quarterly* 8 (Winter 1979): 25–33. Systematic analysis of leftist theater companies by an astute insider.

Forbes, Jill. Review of *Wetherby. Sight and Sound* (Spring 1985): 140. Criticizes the film's reliance upon theatrical contrivances.

Gilbert, W. Stephen. Review of *Plenty. Plays and Players,* June 1978, 28–29. Negative review that faults the absence of "a polemical edge."

Gordon, Giles. Review of *A Map of the World. London Theatre Record* 3 (1983): 48. Judges that the play's meaning does not transcend its structural complexity and ideological characters.

Gussow, Mel. "David Hare: Playwright as Provocateur." *New York Times*

Magazine, 29 September 1985, 42–47, 75–76. Appreciative profile of Hare at the time of the New York production of *A Map of the World.*

———. Review of *Knuckle. New York Times,* 10 March 1981, section C, p. 6. Sees *Knuckle* as shadowboxing and *Plenty* as the main event.

———. "A British Hedda?" *New York Times,* 20 April 1980, Sect. 2, p. 3. Hare's most appreciative American reviewer praises the 1980 Washington, D.C., production of *Plenty* and compares Susan Traherne and Hedda Gabler.

———. Review of *Teeth 'n' Smiles. New York Times,* 14 April 1979, section C, p. 8. Generally favorable review of the 1979 New York production of Hare's "rock play."

Hammond, Jonathan. Review of *Knuckle. Plays and Players,* April 1974, 40–41. Intelligent review of Hare's first production in London's West End.

Holland, Mary. Review of *The Great Exhibition. Plays and Players,* April 1972, 40. Faults the play for its glove-puppet characters and "totally incredible flights of fancy."

Hummler, Richard. "Ruffled Hare Airs Rich Bitch." *Variety,* 15 November 1989, 1. Coverage of the controversy over Rich's review of *The Secret Rapture.*

Kerr, Walter. "Playwrights Are Growing Articulate Again." *New York Times,* 31 October 1981, section 2, p. 3. Favorable notice for the 1982 New York production of *Plenty.*

Kramer, Mimi. Review of *The Secret Rapture. New Yorker,* 13 November 1989, 106, 111–13. Negative review of the New York production.

Kroll, Jack. "The Ladies of London." *Newsweek,* 9 January 1989, 52–53. Favorable notice for the London production of *The Secret Rapture.*

———. Review of *The Secret Rapture. Newsweek,* 13 November 1989, 89. Calls Hare's play "the best play of the year."

Larson, Janet Karsten. Review of *Plenty. The Christian Century,* 23–30 March 1983, 277–78. Insightful and positive review of New York production of *Plenty.*

Leverett, James. Review of *The Secret Rapture. Village Voice,* 7 November 1989, 107. Favorable review of the New York production.

Levin, Bernard. Review of *Plenty. Sunday Times* (London), 16 April 1978, 37. Negative review of the premiere of *Plenty* that criticizes the play as disjointed and oblique.

Lewsen, Charles. Review of *Teeth 'n' Smiles. Times* (London), 3 September 1975, 10. Mixed review of the original London production.

Nightingale, Benedict. Review of *A Map of the World. London Theatre Record* 3 (1983): 48. Extended methodical defense and explanation of the complexity of Hare's play.

Peter, John. "Meet the Wild Bunch." *Sunday Times* (London), 11 July 1976, 31. Profile of Hare, linking him with his contemporaries.

Petley, Julian. Review of *Wetherby. Monthly Film Bulletin* 52 (March 1985): 70–71. Favorable review in the publication of the British Film Society. "Play for Another Day." *Times Educational Supplement* (London), 27 January 1978, 2. Brief account of the censorship controversy surrounding *Scum.*

Ratcliffe, Michael. Review of *The Secret Rapture. Observer,* 9 October 1988, 43. Faults Howard Davies's premiere production while praising Hare's *The Secret Rapture.*

Reed, Rex. Review of *Wetherby. New York Post,* 19 July 1985, 26. Typically obnoxious pan of a film Reed does not understand.

Rich, Frank. Review of *The Knife. New York Times,* 11 March 1987, 24. Largely negative review of Hare's book and direction.

———. Review of *Plenty. New York Times,* 22 October 1983, Section C, p. 3. Unqualified praise for virtually every aspect of the 1982 production of *Plenty* at the New York Shakespeare Festival.

———. Review of *The Secret Rapture. New York Times,* 27 October 1989, sec. C, p. 3. Largely negative review that triggered a controversy over Rich's powers as a reviewer.

Rothstein, Mervyn. "Papp Hastens Uptown Move for Hare's 'Secret Rapture.' " *New York Times,* 29 August 1989, 15. Quotes Papp's objections to the *New York Times'* reviewing policies.

Sarris, Andrew. Review of *Wetherby. Village Voice,* 23 July 1985, 51. One of the few favorable American reviews describes *Wetherby* as "light-years ahead of most contemporary entertainments in maturity, sophistication, and articulateness."

Sterritt, David. Review of *Wetherby. Christian Science Monitor,* 19 July 1985, 23. Generally positive review welcomes "a promising debut film."

Stokes, Geoffrey. "The Secret Rupture." *Village Voice,* 28 November 1989, 37–39. Account of how Jack Kroll was suspended from *Newsweek* in controversy over *The Secret Rapture.*

Stoppard, Tom. "Ambushes for the Audience: Toward a High Comedy of Ideas." *Theatre Quarterly* 4 (1974): 4. Valuable not only for its commentary on Stoppard's early work, but also for its observations on the theatrical climate in Britain in the late 1960s and early 1970s.

Taylor, John Russell. Review of *A Map of the World. Plays and Players,* March 1983, 30–31. Largely unfavorable review sees the play as "cockeyed."

Thomson, David. "Listen to Britain." *Film Comment* 22 (March–April 1986): 56–63. Likens *Wetherby* and *Plenty* to other recent British films.

Turner, John. Review of *The Secret Rapture. Times Literary Supplement* (London), 14–20 October 1988, 1148. Lauds *The Secret Rapture* for its humor and political commentary.

Walker, John. "Top Playwrights." *Sunday Times Magazine* (London), 26 November 1978, 70–71. Schematic "who's who" of British playwrights in the late 1970s.

Wardle, Irving. Review of *Plenty. Times* (London), 13 April 1978, 7. Largely negative review faults *Plenty* as fragmented.

Waterhouse, Robert. Review of *Slag. Plays and Players,* May 1970, 18–19. Praises the cleverness of Hare's comedy, wordplay, and stagecraft.

Wolfe, Matt. "London's Fall Season." *Chicago Tribune,* 13 November 1988, section 13, p. 30. Singles out *The Secret Rapture* as the most successful new play to appear in the fall of 1988.

Yakir, Dan. "Hare Style." *Horizon* 28 (December 1985): 45–47. Overview of Hare's work.

Index